INDIVIDUALIST ESSAYS

GEORGES PALANTE

TRANSLATED BY KIRK WATSON

2nd EDITION

Contents

Contents

TRANSLATOR'S INTRODUCTION

Georges Palante (1862-1925) was a French philosopher, sociologist, and school teacher. He has been ranked among the left-wing disciples of Friedrich Nietzsche, where he joins a pantheon that includes Albert Camus, Emma Goldman, Gilles Deleuze and Michel Foucault (and more recently Michel Onfray, who published a study of Palante's life and thought in 1989).

Palante's obsession is society vis-à-vis the individual. Building on the work of predecessors like Stirner and Nietzsche, he developed an extreme and radical, or one might simply say advanced and subtle, libertarian philosophy: an absolute inoculation against the powers that be, and those that *would* be. Palante was wary of every idea, ideology, morality, tradition, or faith that can be imposed upon the consciousness of the individual to serve the interests of a ruling group or class, or even merely the interests of the group rather than those of its constituent members. In every belief system lie the germs of authoritarianism and the suppression of individual difference. He consistently supported what he called Individualism, but always as a "tendency" rather than a dogma.

In several parts of this collection Palante calls himself a socialist. For him, the only legitimate socialism is a dynamic, responsive form of individualism, defined as "an economic technique, a system of progressive economic experiments" whose only goal must be to open more space for the development of individuals. Although he wrote that "society does not exist: there are only individuals" a full 83 years prior to Margaret Thatcher's well-known speech, Palante's individualism is vastly different from Ayn Rand-inspired "selfishness", which disregards the externalities of individual economic thriving within capitalism. Palante writes that this approach is "a contradictory individualism; it only claims for certain privileged people the integral blossoming of their self, while it becomes an oppressive doctrine for others."

On the other hand, he also critiques the libertarianism and anarchism of the left as naive in its suggestion that after the State has been abolished, individuals will dwell in free societies. In his eyes, society will forever be as much a hindrance to individual flourishing as the State ever was; thus anarchism is utopian and shallow as a critique of existing institutions. "The yoke of social constraint", which will always exist, is more subtle and insidious in its methods of control than the State ever could be. This (socially pessimistic) perspective is incapable of envisioning any truly happy ending for the individual within society or any correct form for it to take; thus the most rewarding part of Palante's writings is his exploration of the realistic options for coping with existence in such a world-view.

This collection can be taken as a sort of tasting platter for Palante's works, since it contains a selection from each of his major works. I hope it will give rise to more interest in Palante's thought.

INDIVIDUAL CONSCIOUSNESS AND SOCIAL CONSCIOUSNESS

From *Précis de sociologie* (1903)

We can now give a clear accounting of the antinomy, — not a superficial, but a real one, — between the individual and the collectivity, the individual consciousness and the social consciousness.

Here we have a dual question. (...) there are points of contact, but also divergences and oppositions between the individual consciousness and the social consciousness. But the oppositions outweigh the harmonies. Let us begin by recognizing the impossibility of absolutely separating the individual consciousness from the social consciousness. The individual, as has been repeated hundreds of times, is not a totality, but an element.

But what is he an element of?

In my view, the individual is less an element of contemporary society, of the social *state* in which he lives, than of the dynamic, ideal society which is developed over time, in which he is only a transitory moment.

In my view, if we truly want to observe the relationship between the individual and society, we should form not a *static* conception, but a dynamic conception, of the latter.

By this I mean that the individual should not look *around himself* to find his orientation and his ideal, but that he should be looking backwards and forwards. He is only a single point in an eternal evolution, but a moving, active, and to a certain extent autonomous point. As Paulhan says:

> The individual is the point of origin for all of those changes whose power so bypasses and almost annihilates him. It is by him, by his inventiveness, that they are transformed; he is the center of this action, whether automatic or voluntary, by which society is protected or transformed. It is he who has the initiative for the changes that will turn the world upside down[1]...

I do not mean to deny the action exercised on the individual by his environment, but we should neither exaggerate this influence nor, above all,

---

[1] Paulhan, *Physiologie de l'Esprit*, p. 176 (Paris, F. Alcan)

set it up, as some do (Spencer, for example), as a precept and a dogma. The individual has the power and right to react against his environment. The latter has no other value or role other than to serve as a point of application and a stimulant for individual energies and to provoke — by reaction, as needed. — the expansion of individuality.

Paulhan continues:

> In certain cases, the individual is correct when he stands against the mob, against the State, against contemporary art, against the science of his contemporaries or against religion. Rembrandt was right versus his contemporaries who ignored him, and Galileo was right vis-a-vis his judges. But in such cases the individual is not only deriving his rights and powers from himself: he represents truths and beauties that are superior to the ones with which he fights. He represents a higher society, greater than the one that oppresses him, like a noble desire randomly sprouting in a brutish soul of a brute, who contemptuously represses it. And this society calls him to do it, and to a certain degree it also carries out the deed.

The points at which the conflict between the individual consciousness and the social consciousness are numerous and important. The social consciousness tends naturally to oppress the individual consciousness. The great social institutions that are called religion, legislative bodies, castes, and classes, tend to subordinate the individual to themselves entirely. But the individual can always react and refuse to allow himself to be absorbed and overrun by the group. The very multiplicity of the social circles in which he participates can be a means of liberation for him, as a means of dominating these social influences, each of which would like to wield exclusive rights over him. He concentrates all of these varied, often antagonistic, influences in his consciousness, and combines them if he has the requisite intellectual energy, in a suitable formula. Here we find Simmel's law of progressive social differentiation. The further evolution advances, the more social circles and social influences are multiplied around the individual; the more it thereby favors his originality and independence. And we arrive at this apparently paradoxical fact that the independence of the individual is a direct factor of the number of social circles in which he participates.

One often finds an antinomy between social progress and the progress of the individual consciousness. But when the progress of society finds itself in contradiction with the progress of the individual, this is only an apparent progress; it is a bogus and ephemeral progress. In fact, it is often a retreat. Societies tend to close off the individual in the pockets of its stationary institutions. By its essence it rejects all that is new and all that is progressive. The individual consciousness is the mother of Progress; it is the mysterious seed carrying the future within, it is like the first primal cell, the obscure and anxious formation of life, carrying in itself the immense genesis of all future lives. Every time any progress has been made, it has been via an individual consciousness. "Men," said Galileo, "are not like horses attached to a carriage, pulling equally: they are like free horses in galloping along, only one of whom will win the trophy." The individual consciousness outshines the social consciousness in clarity and sincerity.

In sincerity, to start. The social consciousness of a given epoch is a web of conventional lies, watchwords that are imposed and shamefully endured[2].

Next, in clarity. The social consciousness is a web of contradictions, which takes quite little reflection to prove. It is, as it were, the dark and

---

[2] See: Max Nordau, *The Conventional Lies of our Civilization* (Paris, F. Alcan).

unthinking part of individual consciousness. In fact, it is not even thought, but is only pseudo-thought by the collective unit. In any social organization, all sorts of principles are invoked as evident truths, and none of their psychological content could ever be embodied in a genuine thought. They are pure psittacisms.

It is the individual consciousness that bursts these lies. This is what, with the weapon of sound logic, resolves all contradictions and annihilates all social psittacisms. The social consciousness, this synthesis of narrow egoisms, lacks all spirit of finesse, strength, and perception, and the independence that allows an individual mind to tackle the problems afflicting life and society. The judgments of groups are necessarily vulgar, massive, and all cut from the same cloth.

A group judges things and men in a unilateral manner, by which I mean that it sees them only from the angle of their *current* utility to the group. If, on a single point a man's attitude has either been or seemed to be in contradiction with the more or less conventional conformity of the group, this man can expect no consideration or even intelligence in the judgments that will be brought against him. This *one*, this impersonal and anonymous force, this *one*, condemns him without appeal and without personal danger, for the judgments of groups enjoy all the irresponsibility cherished by cowardice. The responsibility of each member of the group is swallowed up in its collective impunity.

Such are the judgments of groups, of institutions, of classes, etc. Based on narrow self-interest, on *present* and *near* interests, they are characterized by a lack of meaning in life and by instability. They are permeated by the most complete philistinism. The individual consciousness is able to see past the current interests of society; it has the dynamic sense of life and the future, for it is harmonious and artistic, as life itself is. As Guy de Maupassant writes:

> How often have I observed that the intelligence expands and rises when one lives alone, that it is diminished and lowered when one returns to mix with others! The contacts, all that is said, all one is compelled to hear, to listen to, and answer, have an effect on our own thoughts. A flow and ebb of ideas goes from head to head, and a level is established, an average of intellect is formed from the whole agglomeration of individuals. The qualities of intellectual initiative, wise reflection, and even of the perceptiveness of every isolated man tend to vanish as soon as

they start to mix with a large number of other men[3]."

The reaction of the group swallows the individual's intelligence along with his morality. "Many gatherings of men," says Sighele, "always swallow up, by an inexorable law of collective psychology, the intellectual value of decisions to be taken[4]." As to the nature of the moral influence wielded by the group over the individual, consider this apt observation of Sighele's:

> Notice that when children play together, they become naughtier and more cruel than usual. Roughhousing, swindling, climbing walls: things which none of them would either dare or even think of when alone, become plausible, and even inevitable when they find themselves in company of a few or many. And so we, the adults, must recognize that if we would ever break the laws of delicacy or pity, it is precisely when many of us are together; for the courage for evil then stirs in us, and we find wrongdoing, which we would never consider on our own, a trivial matter[5].

---

[3] Guy de Maupassant, *Afloat* (*Sur l'Eau*).
[4] Sighele, *Psychologie des Sectes*, p. 201.
[5] Sighele, op. cit., p. 215.

In Schopenhauer's view, the social consciousness would be the incarnation of the pure will-to-live, separate from the intellect, of the stupid, ferociously and brutally selfish will-to-live. The individual consciousness is the mysterious hearth where the small flame of liberatory *intelligence* flickers, which elevates the being above the selfishness and ferocity of the will-to-live. It matters little whether we interpret Schopenhauer's view as pessimistic or anything else; as a factual observation, it is conclusive. Since it sees everything from a *static* standpoint, i.e., in light of the group's immediate concerns, the social consciousness is necessarily oppressive and limited; the individual consciousness, which concentrates in itself the intellectual and moral influences which compose this social dynamism, which is developed from one generation to the next, has unlimited horizons in view. It is the mother of the Ideal, the hearth of light and life, the genius of liberation and salvation.

SOCIALISM AND INDIVIDUALISM

From *Précis de sociologie* (1903)

We can now take on the dominant issue of all of Sociology: that is, the relationship between the individual and society. Here we see the two doctrines of socialism and individualism at war.

In a general sense, the word *socialism* points to every social doctrine that subordinates the individual to the collective. This is what "Platonic socialism" refers to. In a more precise and modern sense, socialism is a doctrine which, by an economic reform of the property system, claims to secure increased material and moral independence to the individual.

Individualism is a doctrine which, instead of subordinating the individual to the collectivity, takes as its starting point the idea the individual is an end in himself; that, in both law and in fact, he possesses a particular value and an autonomous existence, and that the social ideal is the most complete liberation of the individual. Understood in this way, individualism is identical with what is still called the libertarian social philosophy.

In a more restricted sense, we understand by "Individualism" the economic theory of *laisser-faire* (the Manchester School). When I speak here of Individualism, I mean individualism understood as a libertarian philosophy.

How do Socialism and Individualism relate to each other?

There are many points of contact between Socialism and Individualism. Socialism is inspired to a great extent by Individualism, and in many respects it tries to fulfill Individualism's ideals. — It proposes to realize the economic emancipation of the individual and seeks to break him free from the clutches of capitalism. And even more: it would like to destroy, not only capitalism as an economic regime, but also the social institutions and foundations which are the consequences of this regime: the capitalistic and bourgeois laws that govern us, the proprietary and *bourgeois* morality that is created by class interests and is oppressive to the individual. A German sociologist has said on this subject:

> Without liberalism, socialism is absolutely inconceivable: socialism is essentially liberal; it is inspired by the ideals of liberation and emancipation which are at present the surest condition and guarantee of his existence. What it works for is nothing less than the emancipation of laborers from the omnipotence of Capital[6].

---

[6] Ziegler, *La Question sociale est une question morale,*

This is not all. Today socialism is yet in a militant phase. It remains a party of opposition and struggle. Thus, it defends liberty in the political, social, and moral realms, whenever it finds occasion. It favors every law, motion, and measure which lead to the material, intellectual, and moral emancipation of the individual. It gleefully seeks to break with the social and moral frameworks of the past. Thus it is that, in the sphere of morality, many socialists are advocates of free love. Thus, in Germany, the entire Socialist Party recently voted against the vexatious and not a little ridiculous Lex Heinze. Thus, it is incontestable that today socialism represents Individualism and is its most powerful social incarnation. Jean Jaurès has highlighted this truth very well in his article "Socialisme et Liberté[7]".

But will it always be thus? When it achieves power, when it holds political sway, will socialism remain liberal and individualistic?

That is the real question, because that is when the germs of anti-individualism that exist in socialism will develop to maturity.

What are these germs?

There are some which are obvious and on which Socialism's adversaries have long focused. Let us

Paris, F. Alcan, p.11
[7] *Revue de Paris*, 1 Dec. 1898

cite for example the probable mania for administration and regulation beyond all need; the ever-increasing claims of society of the right to control what individuals do, the expanding omnipotence of public opinion which, in the socialist regime, will become the principal form of moral sanction. While it's no secret how blind and tyrannical public opinion is, which lends itself to every sort of prejudice; finally, how anti-individualistic it is.

Another point where Socialism seems to be in tension with Individualism is in the unitary dogmatism, or the social and moral monism toward which it always seems to tend. We know, in effect, that many socialists believe in a final monism, that is, an economic and moral uniformization of humanity. Jaurès himself seems to accept this point of view. He speaks of the "great socialist peace", of "the harmony which will burst forth from the clash of forces and instincts[8]." These are nice dreams. But we know also that all social dogmatism and conformity, all unitary social doctrines, are dangerous to individual diversity, to the liberty and independence of the Individual; for all of them require some degree of sacrifice by the Individual in favor of the community. I find a contradiction between Jaurès's individualist point of departure and his goal, namely the final social monism. Departing from libertarian premises, he ends in a kind of social mysticism.

---

[8] *Revue de Paris*, 1 Dec. 1898

Proudhon, whom he called a poet and a sophist, is right in his opposing arguments, where he proclaims the eternity and indestructibility of the basic reality of diversity and struggle within society. At bottom, Jaurès is a Platonist, in spite of his initial individualist inspiration. With him, Socialism reverts to its original form: the subordination of the Individual to the community. — As for myself, I am the resolute adversary of every dogmatism and every social monism because I consider them to be a threat to the Independence of the Individual as well as individual energy. For me, dogmatism and monism are synonymous with absolutism, coercion and constraint. All social and moral dogmatisms have a tendency to become tyrannical. And this is why Nietzsche was right to protest against them in the name of the "instinct for beauty" and the "instinct to greatness". These dogmatisms authorize authoritarian control of the individual consciousness by the social consciousness, in the name of so-called infallible rules and the social quarantining of any who contravene these rules. I would not claim that all of these consequences are contained in Jaurès's own socialist conception, but minds that are less liberal than his may draw these conclusions, and they constitute, in the very centre of Socialism, a peril for Individualism.

I must say a word here about the arguments which the partisans of the social dogmatism invoke, by which I mean the doctrine of those who pose the existence of society as prior and superior to that of the Individual.

Two kinds of arguments have been invoked in favor of this dogmatism, some *a priori*, others *a posteriori*. And we may thus distinguish two sorts of social dogmatisms: social dogmatisms *a priori* and social dogmatisms *a posteriori*.

The social dogmatism *a priori* has as its principal and original representative Plato, remains the eternal spokesman of the unitary social philosophy. Plato, as is well known, invokes the rational idea of unity, and he believes that this idea hovers above Individuals, that it is anterior and superior to them. Consequently, the city is superior to the citizens. The city is all; the individual is nothing. Aristotle has done away with this argument. Refuting Plato, he shows that a logical deduction of the idea of unity will lead us to divinize the individual rather than the city:

> In effect, Socrates sees absolute unity as the end goal of the city. But what is a city? It is a multitude made up of diverse elements; make it more unitary, and your city becomes a family; centralize further, and your family will be concentrated on the individual: for there is more unity in the family than in the city and more still in the individual than in the family[9].

---

[9] Aristotle, *Politics*, Book II

Thus, no unity is more real or complete than the Individual. Thus, it is the he who, by Plato's own principles, would best incarnate the idea of unity. It is also by means of an *a priori* that certain Kantians and neo-Kantians arrive at their *a posteriori* social dogmatism, thinking they can affirm the necessary and legitimate subordination of the individual to society. But their arguments have no more value than the Platonic argument which we find to some extent in all the others.

The *a posteriori* social dogmatists claim to base this subordination on a fact of experience, generalized and interpreted as a natural necessity. This is the method of those who subordinate the Individual to society in the name of the law of adaptation to the environment or the law of symbiosis (Izoulet) or, again, the law of solidarity, and so on.

These philosophers' theories could be classed under the general heading of *historicism* (to use Nietzsche's expression). For they regard the Individual as a mere resultant, a mere reflection of his historical environment.

It was against this historicism that Nietzsche protested. It is he who, more vigorously than any other thinker, tried to shake off this net that they tried to cast over his head, whose meshes are called: "environment", "heredity", "tradition", "conventional morality".

Nietzsche is right. These philosophers set up the absolute passivity and nothingness of the Individual a dogma. They forget that the individual is himself a force, an important factor of his environment, and that he can transform it just as much as he can passively adapt himself to it. "It is true," said Scipio Sighele, "that men of genius are more than actors, that they are the authors of the human drama[10]." But this can be applied, controlling for proportions, to every human individual. Recall the distinction that we set up between the *static* and *dynamic* standpoints from which to envision society. If, from the static point of view, i.e., in *a given moment of evolution*, the environment imposes an inevitable limit on the activities of the Individual, then from the dynamic standpoint, i.e., from the standpoint of social evolution and ascension, the Individual regains his rights. For he is, from this standpoint, the source of initiative, the agent of progress, the mover of history.

Rejecting all forms of social dogmatism, as well as dogmatism *a posteriori* as well as dogmatism *a priori*, we set up Individualism as the true social philosophy.

We can now see clearly what is true and what is false in socialism.

---

[10] S. Sighele, *Psychologie des Sectes*, p. 224

Socialism is legitimate and true insofar as it struggles for the ideals of liberty and individual emancipation. As such, *it is only a stage in the development of individualism.* And it is legitimate to the extent that it is an affirmation of Individualism.

But socialism is wrong if it thinks it can remain immobile with a stationary dogma, in a unitary conception, in a fixed ideal, if it becomes yet another social dogmatism. For then it assumes the character of every dogmatism: that of being a compulsion and a constraint for the Individual. Many socialists have glimpsed this danger and have properly refused to encapsulate socialism in any definitive, dogmatic formulation. In an article[11] written *a propos* of the death of Nietzsche, E. Gystrow rejects socialism as an immobile and static conception, and only legitimizes a dynamic socialism that is constantly evolving, constantly overcoming itself. He said further:

> That old revolutionary, Engels himself, made a blank slate of the obligatory revolution. The movement of socialism toward its *end-goal* (*Endziel*) should be accomplished by legal means. Then came Bernstein, who excised the dogma of the *end-goal* altogether... Every movement has a direction; but a direction and an end-goal are completely different things.

---

[11] *Sozialistische Monatshefte,* Oct 1900

A historical movement is not a defined line, a parabola, or an Archimedean spiral, but a curve which the more clever analytical geometricians will try to plot in vain. There are no end-goals in history which, in the very moment of its attainment, cannot be transcended. No end-goal can ever be more than a provisional point in the direction of the movement. In its progress toward the final goal, the historical movement keep moving it along. What we call the ideal of a movement is not in its final term; rather, it accompanies it in every instant and is displaced along with it: it proceeds along with it like the pillar of fire with the camp of Israel. So long as a historical movement sets itself an end-goal in the proper sense of the term, it is immature; it persists in childish dreaming. Doubtless, this phase is necessary. But just as the child will grow up, the day will come when the historical movement must laugh at its childish fancies. If a movement lasts this long, this itself is the touchstone of its right to existence. Socialism has cast its *end-goal* overboard; instead it possesses an ideal which, instead of being in front of it, is found inside it and makes its imprint on it.

I, too, repudiate any socialism that comes in a dogmatic and immobile form. But I allow for the possibility of a dynamic socialism, a socialism in eternal state of becoming, a socialism that is both carried and created by individual wills instead of imposing itself on them; in a word, a socialism that is identical with Individualism.

But as I mentioned, this socialism must escape the dangerous illusion of social monism. It must also transcend the illusion of absolute equality.

There is one inequality that can be suppressed: that of classes; but there is one that cannot be done away with: that of individuals.

We may be able to suppress the conventional social hierarchies, but not the personal ascendancy of minds. As Henri Mazel said, "there will always be active and passive people, energetic men and madmen[12]."

By this, we can see in Gystrow's paradox — the reconciliation of Nietzscheanism and socialism — is not as indefensible as it seems at first glance.

Indeed, although Nietzsche was attracted to aristocracy, he is not as far from socialism as we may think. First, he claimed the right of anyone to become an aristocrat. The Nietzschean maxim: "Not only onward shalt thou propagate thyself, but upward!" can become that of socialism and of democracy altogether. For, Nietzsche proclaimed the true principle of all true socialism and of all democracy: the infinite value and worth of the person. He courageously repudiated the illusion of a final monism, of universal conformity and peace in the heart of a dogma brought to fruition. That kind of peace would only represent stagnation and torpor.

---

[12] Mazel, *La Synergie sociale*, p. 348

Today, many socialists[13], following Gystrow, are drawing closer to this standpoint.

> One finds links between Nietzsche and socialism: a loathing for sentimentality, for the odious whiff of the peace-pipe. And both hold their nose at the odor drifting in from the common kitchens where the soups are boiling, waiting to be consumed in common, the gruel of harmony... It is only by struggle that personality is enlarged. One workers' strike stirs more individuality than volumes full of bombast about "self-improvement", etc.

> The possession of power costs dear — power makes you stupid — but the struggle for power is the vital principle of every great movement, and it is enough for us that in it and by it individualities rise up, more numerous and wealthy than ever... Once, socialism was a dogma. Today, it is a great movement. The dogma falls to pieces; but the sensibility and the individual life are more fertile and rich than ever.

---

[13] While correcting the proofs for this work, I have in hand a recent article on Socialism, in which the author focuses on the perennial nature of individualism and on the need for individual energy and responsibility, even and especially in the center of all economic cooperation. I find this suggestive formula here: "For the evolutionary socialists, socialism will never be; *it will only become...*" (J. Sarraute, *Socialisme d'opposition, socialisme de gouvernement et lutte de classe. Revue socialiste*, Dec. 1900)

Nietzsche was one of ours. He was not the philosopher of the Romanticism looking back to the medieval corporations, and he broke off relations with Wagner, who was, in art, the representative of this Romanticism. No more was he the philosopher of capitalism... He believed in the great men of the past and — this is what is most admirable and divine in this genius — in the *great humanity* of the future. He prophesied what should be the principle of our task: that the value of humanity resides in man himself, and that every true ascent of humanity will have an aristocratic direction[14]...

Yes, there is no true democracy without an aristocratization of the mob. A friend of mine once proposed to read and comment on the section on the "rope-dancer" from *Thus Spake Zarathustra*, to a crowd. He was discouraged from this reading do to its nature as little democratic and full of contempt for the mob. Still, my friend was in the right. The mob must be ennobled, and dislodged from its mob-mentality; that it sense the horror of that abominable gregarious spirit that Nietzsche so admirably exposed:

> Get out of this town, O Zarathustra; they who hate you are too many. The good and the just hate you, and they call you their enemy and despiser; the devout hate you, and they call you a danger to the mob. It was your good

[14] Gystrow, "Etwas ueber Nietzsche und uns Sozialistischen," in *Socialistische Monatshefte*

fortune to be mocked; for truly you spoke as a buffoon. It was your pleasure to associate with the dead dog: by lowering yourself in this way you remained alive, for today. But go out of this town — or tomorrow, I will leap over you[15].
..

We are now equipped understand the true relations of the collectivity and the individual. Doubtless, some truth is contained in this verse of Goethe's:

> *Wie viel bist du von andern unterschieden?*
> *Erkenne dich, leb' mit der Welt in Frieden[16].*

But neither should we misunderstand the real inequalities and diversity that exist among individuals. We must not underestimate the need for struggle in order to create the ideal, to sculpt the personality.

At bottom, there is no contradiction between aristocratic individualism and democratic individualism. To glorify the great, the free individualities, is to prepare ourselves for glorifying *all* human personalities, in that they are capable of liberty and greatness. One of Gabriel Tarde's laws ("the law of passing from unilaterality to reciprocality") might be useful here, to explain this passing from aristocratic individualism to democratic individualism.

---

[15] *Thus Spake Zarathustra*, §8
[16] How different are you from others? / Know yourself, and live at peace with the world.

Carlyle said: "I see the blessedest result preparing itself: not abolition of Hero-worship, but rather what I would call a whole World of Heroes. If Hero means a sincere man, why may not every one of us be a Hero[17]?"

The enemy, the true threat to our democracy, is not the individualist theory of great men, but every theory which, in the name of a any principle whatsoever, in the name of any dogma whatsoever, would abandon individual initiative, individual action to the gregarious spirit.

This gregarious spirit must be got rid of. We must be liberated from this need for spineless and cowardly sociability, this scourge of modern life. A man must know how to be himself, how to live in himself, and by himself alone.

Consider Pascal's words: "Let us contemplate our salvation": our terrestrial salvation, which is nowhere but in the independence and mastery of the self. Maybe this is selfishness. But, if there is selfishness in it, this simple and frank selfishness is better than that complicated and bloated selfishness of social hypocrisy which certain people advocate under the guise of solidarity, symbiosis, etc.

And above all, no dogmas, no protection, no social guardianship of the individual. The gods

---

[17] Translator's note: See Thomas Carlyle, *On Heroes, Hero-Worship, and the Heroic in History*: Lectures on Heroes, Lecture IV.

are dead, the religions are dead. The conventional moral and social dogmas are all dying. The human individual can and should count on nothing but himself. It is free thought and free action, "the arrow of desire towards the far shore"[18].

Nietzsche has admirably rendered this feeling in terms that recall a few magnificent lines from Jean-Marie Guyau's *Sketch of a Morality without Sanction or Obligation*. In both we find the same arrogant, stoic, prophetic emphasis: the same breeze from the future enlivening the atmosphere:

> We other philosophers and free spirits, at the news that the old God is dead, we feel ourselves illuminated by a new dawn; our hearts overflow with recognition, astonishment, apprehension and waiting — finally, the horizon seems freed again, even while we confess that it remains unclear — finally our vessels can again set sail, drifting into danger; once again, all the perils for those who seek knowledge are allowed; the sea, our full sea opens again before us, and maybe there never was such a *full* sea[19].

> He who enters this immense, almost new domain of dangerous knowledge will suffer from such a view of things as from sea-sickness. And, in fact, there are a hundred good reasons for everyone to keep away when

---

[18] Nietzsche, *Thus Spake Zarathustra*, §8
[19] Nietzsche, *The Joyful Wisdom*

they can! On the other hand, when he has wrecked his bark, well then, onward! Grit our teeth! Open our eyes! Firm hand to the helm! We will go beyond morality, we will understand, we may crush our own reserves of morality, going as we do, venturing as we will in this direction—but what does that matter! Never was a more *profound* world ever revealed in to the eyes of intrepid voyagers and adventurers[20]...

---

[20] Nietzsche, *Beyond Good and Evil*, §23

THE SOCIAL DOGMATISMS AND THE LIBERATION OF THE INDIVIDUAL

From *Combat pour l'individu* (1904)

There are two possible conceptions of the way the individual and society relate to each other. The partisans of the social dogmatisms think that the individual, considered either in his origins or his nature, or in his end, is but an element and nearly an epiphenomenon of society. The supporters of individualism, on the other hand, regard each individual as a small and separate world, with its own existence and an independent originality. In the first conception, society is seen as having a prior and superior value to the individual, and any rights he might claim against society are curtailed. In the second conception, the individual has his own value, along with rights which can under no circumstances be sacrificed for social ends.

I would like to draw attention to the inanity of every social dogmatism. This task would seem to be the indispensable propaedeutic for the liberation of the individual.

But before I begin, allow me to clarify a few things. For me, the problem does not lie between the individual and the State, but between the individual and society. Herbert Spencer wrote his book *Man versus the State* in hopes of liberating the individual from statist tyranny. One might entitle another book *Man versus Society*, to liberate the individual from social tyrannies. Spencer's individualism is only a false individualism. It is true that he would free the individual from the yoke of the State, but he leaves him as bowed as ever beneath the yoke of social constraint, against which he can only envision man to have a certain capacity to adapt to the situation. Spencer grants man, at bottom, only a basic receptiveness without initiative of his own.

The State's constraints are one thing, and those of society are another. Statist constraints are summed up as the law that is promulgated and the public force that sanctions it. That is simple and plain. The social restraints are far more complicated. Also more hypocritical. They fetter the individual with a thousand small, invisible ties: the self-interest and the passions of the group, the class, the clan, the corporation, etc.; they bend him with a thousand small customs, a thousand clichés, conventional praise and blame, all aiming to transform him into a good herdling.

Here the brutal openness of the legal Imperative is replaced by hypocrisy practiced by a group, with sheeplike discipline on all sides, a universal tactic of concerted subjugation and of mutual spying which has found its most repulsive and formidable expression in the *Monita secreta*, that charter of a certain Illustrious Company[21], but which is created by something like spontaneous generation and becomes applied of its own accord in every human herd. And from this perspective we may say that the morality of the *Monita secreta* is only a mirror that exaggerates the traits of all gregarious morality, as it functions in a class, a clan, or a group.

The individual is often the unwitting accomplice of this conspiracy against his liberty. He fashions for himself, at first glance, an illusion of the benefits he derives from his affiliation with the group. It seems to him that his individual will-to-live, his vital drives are exalted; that his personal will-to-power is extraordinarily intensified by the fact of fusing with the egoism of the group. He fails to see that by being absorbed into the collective will-to-live, he denies himself as a *self*. He will be all the more easily taken in by this gregarious illusion to the extent that his *self* is intellectually and morally weak. Schopenhauer make a fine remark that many men, in the absence of personal merits that encourage self-esteem, find pride in the group to which they belong. "This cheap pride betrays the person who attains it in the absence of individual qualities; for without it he would not have recourse to what

---

[21] Translator's note: This was a forged document purporting to be a secret communication for the Jesuits, aiming to increase their power by devious means.

he shares with so many individuals[22]." To the extent that an individual lacks self regard, he is easily absorbed by a group. With such a man, personal tastes, ideas, passions, and watchwords, will soon cease to be anything but the derivatives of the tastes, ideas, passions and watchwords dominant within the group. Here the collective will-to-live hovers above the individual wills in the same way that the genius of the species is not only an addition to individual wills; it has its own laws, its particular aims. To secure its victory, the individual wills are themselves annihilated with the same naive unwitting as the good young man described in the *Monita Secreta*, who will be induced little by little into the preferred paths, entangled gradually in the net, from which he'll never be able to escape.

The individualist protest against the State does not get to the bottom of the matter. The individualist's real fight is against the anti-individualist influences *par excellence*, those hypocritical and mute influences that act in the dark domain of self-interest and group passions.

The promulgated law is only the abstract, faded, and intellectualized expression of collective influences. By becoming intellectualized, these influences lose something of their primitive, gregarious ferocity; they have been dressed up with a semblance of impassable serenity, of impersonal indifference. This is what translates

---

[22] Schopenhauer, *Wisdom in Life*

the word *justice*, which carries a sense of absolute impartiality. But, as Remy de Gourmont has established, at bottom, justice never exists in a pure and abstract state. In its real-world application, it depends on diverse interpretations which various social groups give regarding their own ideas of *good* and *evil*.

The law is a reflection of custom. It is oppressive to the extent to which a society's customs are barbaric, with the reservation already given, that the law always contains a degree of collective ferocity. The gregarious virus is attenuated by the enlargement of its sphere of influence. The law, impersonal and abstract, worn out by overuse, is to custom — constrained, passionate, and hateful — that which the concept — the worn-out image — is to the perceptible image before its effacement, to the colorful and vivid concrete image. Thus, the individual is taken in by an illusion whenever he hopes to find in the State and in Justice any assistance against the blind decrees of groups. In fact, there is a pre-established harmony between the two series of constraints. Statist authority typically betrays, or at least abandons, the individual to any gregarious hatreds that pursue him. Its decisions confirm and sanction, on a larger scale, the volitions of this omnipotent power: the selfishness of the group.

We have thus posed the problem of the contradiction of the individual and society in all its generality. I resolve this contradiction fully in favor of the individual. Let us see how and why.

To begin, we must distinguish between two kinds of social dogmatisms: the dogmatisms *a priori* and the dogmatisms *a posteriori*.

Among the dogmatic philosophers, in effect, some have proceeded *a priori* and have claimed to establish, via mere logical deduction, the self-existence of, and the superior value of, society. A great number of thinkers have followed this method, from Plato to Hegel. Others have attempted to justify *a posteriori* the superior rights of society by examining the life-conditions to which men are subject by reason of their physiological and psychological makeup. They have developed Aristotle's aphorism: "Man is the political animal", and have shown that the factual conditions in which human life is developed, make society into a superior and necessary law, against which no individual either can or should try to struggle. The representatives of the *a posteriori* or naturalist social dogmatisms are equally numerous in the history of thought, from Aristotle to the modern theorists of society-as-organism, to the theorists of cooperation or solidarity, as well as the defenders of the gregarious social philosophy.

The social dogmatisms, in these two forms, seem to respond to one of the demands of the social will-to-live. In effect, every organized social group appears to feel an instinctive need to legitimize itself in the eyes of the individuals who constitute it. Not content to impose social discipline by force, they prefer to have the legitimacy of their discipline accepted, to have it taken as just and rational. In the beginning, Religion was asked to bless social discipline as sacred; later the philosophers were asked, who rarely lack for convenient formulas to rationalize Force. They generally agree with Hegel's view, for whom "what is real is rational". Let me note that in the social dogmatism *a priori*, it is the State which they seek to justify, representing it as the incarnation of a rational idea. "The State is an expression, a fancied reality of a people[23]."

In the social dogmatism *a posteriori*, the idea is to justify the social mechanism in its entirety; i.e., in the complexity of the social discipline which it imposes on the individual.

Let us examine first of all the social dogmatism *a priori*.

While taking up this line of thought, we find that it carries a distinction: we can distinguish between a *transcendent* rationale which places in the metaphysical heavens of the Immutable, the principle which confers reality upon societies, and a rationale of *Immanence*, which places it in the world of the change and progress. In addition, in both cases we proceed *a priori*; in

---

[23] Lazarus and Steinthal, *Jahrschrift für Völkerpsychologie*, p. 10

both cases we are subordinating facts to Ideas, the Real to the Logical.

The oldest form of the *transcendent* social dogmatism is found in Plato. For this philosopher, the State has an absolute right over individuals. The unity of the City should be seen as a symbol of the ideal or divine unity. Individuals are only amorphous material, upon which the City confers the dignity of particular forms. In this respect, the State only has rights, the individual only has duties.

Another form of the transcendental social dogmatism is what we find in certain Kantians, as well as in Kant himself. We know that there are, in the Kantian social morality, two tendencies which are hard to reconcile. On one hand, Kant sets up the human person as an end in himself and thereby seems to incline towards individualism. On the other hand, by his conception of an absolute and rational moral law, he ends with a moral universalism, which poses rules as prior and superior to individuals. The role of individuals is only to serve as instruments for the law. This latter plane, which is transcendental, hovers above individual consciences, or rather is personified in the State and its administrators. The City, the State become the symbol of the transcendent moral law, and as such, like the moral law itself, are invested with superior rights.

Kant's individualism here converts into a moral-metaphysical doctrine that sets up the State as an end in itself. Auguste Burdeau, one of the interpreters of this later Kantian philosophy, has written: "We do not have the right to withdraw from the service of the State any fraction of our fortune, any effort of our arms, any thought from our intelligence, any drop of our blood, any beating of our hearts[24]."

The same conclusion is found with Mr. Johann Fichte, with whom the theory of the absolute Self leads to a unitary theory of the State. It is likewise found with Dorner, who is currently a philosopher and professor in the University of Königsberg. He sees the State as a symbol of Absolute Spirit; according to him, the individual is attached to corporations; by these to the State, and by the latter to Absolute Spirit[25].

The Platonic and Kantian social Dogmatism will rightly feel outdated to many people. May we in good faith attribute to the State, to Society, some supra-sensible value, as Plato does? The modern conscience, no friend to transcendentalism, will doubtless find such things harder and harder to conceive.

The State, said Plato, is a symbol of Divine Unity. Aristotle left us a nice phrase, which did justice to this wretched idea:

---

[24] Cited by Barrès, *Les Déracinés*, p. 21
[25] Dorner, *Das menschliche Handeln*, p. 461

Socrates praised the idea of an absolute unity of the City. But what is a City? It is a multitude composed of diverse elements; give it more unity, and your City becomes a family; centralize it further, your family is concentrated in the individual: for there is more unity in the family than in the city, and more still in the individual than in the family[26].

Thus, there is no unity more real or complete than what we find in the individual. Then it is the individual who, according to Plato's own principles, best embodies the idea of unity.

But the unity of the State is a myth. Max Nordau asks:

> What is the State? Speaking theoretically, this should be: You and Me. But in practice it is a dominant class, a small number of personalities, often a single person. To place the stamp of the State on everything, is to do pleasure to a single class exclusively, certain people only, even a single person[27].

Count Gobineau said likewise:

> The experience of all ages has shown that there is no worse tyranny than that which is exercised for the benefit of fictions, beings who are by nature insensible, pitiless and infinitely shameless in their pretensions. Why? Because these fictions, themselves incapable of looking out for their own

---

[26] Aristotle, *Politics*, Book 2
[27] *Paradoxes sociologiques*, p. 125

interests, delegate their powers to deputies. The latter, since they are not expected to act selfishly, acquire the right to commit the greatest of atrocities. They are always innocent when they strike in the name of the idol whose priests they claim to be[28].

What symbolic link might exist between the Platonic Idea and human societies? The features of the Platonic Idea are, as is well known, purity, simplicity, the ideal and luminous truth. These features would be translated by the simplicity and sincerity of social relations in the heart of the State.

To begin with, the State is less a plastic principle relative to social relations in general than a result and an epiphenomenon of the latter. Moreover, the social consciousness, even informed by the State, is far from presenting any such features of simplicity, logic and sincerity. If this is obvious for us, it is because the social conscience of an era, a web of unseen contradictions and dissimulated lies, is inferior in this regard to even a mediocre individual conscience, because this latter can, at least sometimes, make an effort at consistency and being true to its own nature. And with the mechanism set in motion, claiming its actions are inspired by the drive to bring the Idea to victory, only adds new insincerities to those which already existed.

---

[28] Gobineau, *De l'Inégalite des races humaines*, Volume II. p. 31

Likewise, what symbolic link exists between the ideal moral law of the Kantians and human societies? The defining characteristic of this law is absolute disinterestedness. The State is only a utilitarian organization, which Schopenhauer has defined so well as the masterpiece of collective selfishness. The city is only the most perfect form of the human will-to-live. It is this will-to-live, condensed and carried to its maximum concentration. Yet the will-to-live, which is expressed in the acts of the individual life or in those of social life, is foreign, if not rebellious, against morality. It is amoral. Consequently, the city, the simple maker of human bliss, no more resembles the law of absolute disinterestedness than the flower in your garden resembles the sun shining in the skies. In his criticism of Fichte's morality, Schopenhauer said quite correctly:

> To judge everything by this moral apparatus, nothing would be more important than society: how? Nobody can find out. All we can see is that, if bees require association to build cells and a hive, in men there must be some apparent need of association, a need to participate in an immense, strictly moral drama, which embraces the whole universe, where we are marionettes and nothing more. The sole, but essential, difference is that the hive has some use, while the moral drama of the universe is, in reality, very immoral indeed[29].

---

[29] Schopenhauer, *On the Basis of Morality*

With these social philosophies, the abyss between theory and practice is unbridgeable. One fails to see how the social, ethical and political monism of the Platonists and Kantians will be brought down to Earth. For them, the State is a formal unity, externally imposed upon a diverse social multiplicity, which is to some extent resistant against unity. Yet who will assure us that unity will finally gain the upper hand over diversity? No society is unitary. Every society is composed of diverse societies in mutual conflict. And far from diminishing in course of evolution, these conflicts, according to Simmel, always become more accentuated and diversified.

I conclude, then, that nothing is less evident than the social dogmatism of the transcendental metaphysicians.

Let us pass on to what we have called the social dogmatism of Immanence. The representatives of this social philosophy come more or less directly from Hegelianism. — For Hegel, the ruling idea in social evolution is no longer a divine and transcendent idea. The principle he invokes is no longer Plato's Reason-in-Actuality, but a Reason-in-Motion, a living and moving harmony, made up of contraries, which itself seeks realization and is gradually realized. Hegel, as is well known, derived from this an authoritarian social dogmatism which ends up serving as a defense for the Prussian monarchy, which he considered to be the summit of dialectical historical ascension. This dogmatism became more liberal with Hegel's disciples. In a general way, the social dogmatism of the philosophy of progress is less rigid than the social dogmatism of the transcendentalists. — This dogmatism leaves more room for the individual. The conception of the identity of contraries erases every limit set between good and evil and ends by viewing them as historical categories. The revolutionary character of the Hegelian far-left is not in doubt. Mr. Eugène de Roberty, who is attached to this school on some points, says that "the free criticism of the norms that regulate human conduct or that which is commonly called disrespect, irreverence, or even 'moral skepticism', is the necessary condition of all progress in ethical knowledge and even in morality[30]."

The Hegelian philosophy, even with its far-left representatives, remains a metaphysical dogmatism, and consequently a moral and social dogmatism. The Hegelian philosophy is dogmatic by its affirmation of the primacy of intelligence over instinct (Panlogism), an affirmation that translates into sociology as the tendency to place knowledge at the beginning of all social development and at the bottom of the series of social values. There is the point of view adopted by, for example, de Roberty, in opposition to the Marxist standpoint, who would rather place, with Julius Lippert, a "drive to find

---

[30] *Constitution de l'Ethique,* p. 90

favorable living-conditions[31]" at the root of the social process. The Hegelian philosophy is also dogmatic in its affirmation of an ultimate social monism, of the inexorable advent of altruism and the final absorption of the individual psychism into the collective one. De Roberty repudiates agnosticism and wants to "go beyond God". In spite of his denials it is hard not to find a new metaphysics in these theses. And, as liberal as his tendencies may be, I fear that this metaphysical dogmatism may convert into a social dogmatism bearing as its natural fruit the subordination of the individual to society, of egoism to altruism.

Yet, the Panlogism of immanence, with its consequences: monism and ultimate altruism, is no more scientifically true than the theses of the transcendental metaphysicians. The shadow is only displaced. The logical idols: Unity and Truth can come down from Heaven to Earth all they like, but they'll be idols still. It is always the same recurring illusion which, despite the Kantian lesson in his *Critique of Pure Reason*, poses relativities as absolutes, and brings the whole fantastic mythology of Morality back for minds that are servile.

I believe that the inanity of these social dogmatisms, resting on Logic, has now been demonstrated well enough. I pass to those which

---

[31] *Lebensfuersorge*

appeal to experience. The latter are summed up in a single word and ideal: namely, "solidarity".

Allow me to distinguish between several forms of solidarity: "genetic" or "organic" solidarity; "economic" solidarity; "intellectual" solidarity; "moral" and "social" solidarity. Note that each of these forms of solidarity have been invoked as the basis of a social dogmatism.

"Genetic" or "organic" solidarity refers to the dependence of the individual on its parents, and in a general manner on its species. In the name of this solidarity, Alfred Espinas, in a recent article frankly anti-individualist in inspiration[32], denies the individual as an independent and autonomous agent. The individual, he says, is only an abstraction: the group alone is a real being. The group is, at least, based on genetic linkages. "The only societies that can be considered as beings are those whose members are united by all the connections of Life, including reproduction and education, which bring union about by means of nutrition itself. A group without families would not be a society." The family is the nucleus of the city. Familial solidarity is the fundamental social link. And it is biology that teaches us a natural and necessary subordination of the individual to the society or the species.

---

[32] "Être ou ne pas être, ou du postulat de la Sociologie," *Revue Philosophique,* May 1901

The facts the Espinas alleges are too obvious to require any special focus by him. But I can't say the same for his conclusions.

It is true that the individual cannot extricate himself from the laws of generation any more than from the laws of gravity. But does this mean that the individual has no role except to be an agent of transmission of the specific type, whether ethnic or familial; no law other than strict compliance with the social conditions best suited to guarantee the life and preservation of the group: either the family, the city, or the species?

Doubtless, the biological issue regarding human individuality is a difficult problem. Espinas has shown elsewhere[33] how difficult it is to determine at what precise moment the individuality of the infant is divided from that of its mother to form an independent unity. As close as the fusion of the two existences may be, the moment will always come when a separation occurs. From this original fact: the genetic and organic solidarity that unites the child to its parents and to those who have cared for it during the dependent phase of its existence, Espinas thinks he can deduce all other relations that make up the individual's life. But surely this is simplifying things to extremes. There can be no rules as rigid as those of animal societies. In humanity, a thousand familial formulations,

---

[33] "Congers de Paris," *Annales*, p. 321

either political, or social, are possible. These combinations and their unending variations are, by and large, the effect of individual initiative, that is to say, the aspirations, desires, passions, even the revolts which traverse individual souls. And thus for each individual, upon his entry into life, an immense domain of relativities and contingencies is opened up, in which his personal will-to-live can start moving in its own way. For example, historically the types of family organization (patriarchy, matriarchy, polyandry, polygamy, monogamy, etc.) have been quite diverse; entirely different kinds of political and social organization have both existed and prospered. All of them took shape and evolved under pressure from conditions where genetic solidarity may have played a role, but where other important factors were also crucial.

To subordinate the individual to a given social organization in the name of "genetic" solidarity is to forget that in all aspects of social organization, artifice mingles with nature. In our social organizations the conventional lies, the "untruths", in Nietzsche's term, superimpose themselves on the simple natural facts of human generation, and lay their fantastic and tyrannical scaffolding upon the docile herd. To set up as a dogma this social phantasmagoria, to proclaim it sacrosanct to the individual in the name of the simple genetic linkage that binds the individual to the species, is to be too hasty. Why not end all at once, like Hegel, with the declaration that marriage is a "sacred duty", and divinize the social forces embodied in modern bourgeois marriage: the omnipotent and comic "Lady" as described by Schopenhauer?

The truth is that the organic solidarity which binds the individual to the species in no way excludes the possibility of individual initiative, in morality and society, and in this way of action exerted by the individual himself on the future of the species. There is a hypothesis in which the influence of the individual upon the species is null, from the organic, psychological, moral and social point of view. This is Weismann's hypothesis on the non-transmissibility of "inherited traits". Individual variations have no influence over the future of the species. The individual is but a simple agent for the transmission of unalterable, germinal plasma. But we know that the most authoritative biologists, Le Dantec for example, tend definitively to reject this theory. "Individualization," said Mr. Le Dantec, "allows an acquired perfection under the influence of certain environmental conditions that fix themselves into the heredity of the species; this is the only means by which nature can realize progressive evolution[34]." Thus the individual is an agent, and the only agent, of progress. From the social perspective, these are the thousands of infinitesimal actions by human individualities over the course of time, these are the thousands

---

[34] Le Dantec, "La Definition de l'individu," *Revue philosophique*. Feb. 1901

of experiences tending toward an expansion of happiness and liberty, for which individual initiative has been the point of departure, and which, at length, constitute what we call the progress of the species. Let us give the individual his due.

After the "genetic" solidarity, "economic" solidarity is invoked as a basis of social dogmatism.

How exactly should this solidarity be understood? The solidarists themselves feel the need to find out the meaning of this word that they use so often: "By drawing up the catechism of the Ligue de l'education sociale," says Charles Gide, "we ourselves notice that we failed to understand in a very precise fashion exactly what this solidarity is, into which we want to bring others[35]." Truly, no concept begs for elucidation more than solidarity. The word solidarity, in the jargon of economics, is rendered as the division of labor and as the exchange of values or services. Outside of this exact and verifiable signification in political economy, the senses that this word can take on are quite vague. Gide, making an effort to enlarge the concept of solidarity, comes to identify solidarity with altruism. Speaking of the concept of solidarity among the economic liberals, he said:

---

[35] *Conference faite au cercle des etudiants liberaux de Liege*, 3 May 1901

What miserable solidarity is the cash nexus! It excludes everyone who has been overlooked, having nothing to contribute. They are numerous, and yet, these Robinsons of society, who lack even the recovered debris from the shipwreck, waiting in vain for the ship that will bring them back to their fellows... For such, both the division of labor and exchange are meaningless. ...True solidarity strives to make this word, which is so often repeated, a reality: *nos semblables*[36]. It aims at the unity of fragmented humanity, which must be reconstituted. It speaks through the mouth of Victor Hugo, saying: "What a madman, to believe that you and I are not the same", or by Carlyle in his parable of the poor Irish widow who said to her lifelong companions: "I am your sister, bone of your bone; the same God made us both", or by Jesus when praying: "Father, may they all be one in me[37]!"

Thus, just like that, solidarity is now one with charity, but is charity a part of economics? Can it even become part of it?

In fact, it is selfishness sets all economic activities in motion. Gide cites the cooperative associations as an example of solidarity extended in the manner he had spoken of. But the associations of cooperation, of mutuality, etc., are enterprises of enlightened self-interest. The proof if this is that as soon as the participants

---

[36] Translator's footnote: a play on the two meanings of this term: "our fellows" and "those who are like us"

[37] *Recherche d'une définition de la Solidarité*, p. 15

think they see their interests at risk, they pull out of these associations. It is likely that, in spite of the efforts of the solidarists and the preaching of the moralists, this will be the case for a long time yet. When Gide invokes charity, or rather altruism, he leaves economics and starts talking about morality. He transforms economic solidarity into moral solidarity. Charity, fraternity, altruism: all fine ideas. Cabet has already invoked them. Proudhon responded very well to him, saying that fraternity cannot, in economics, be a point of departure, but only a destination. He wrote:

> For anyone who has reflected on the progress of human sociability, effective fraternity, heartfelt and rational fraternity, which alone deserves the care of the legislator and the attention of the moralist, and of which racial fraternity is only its fleshly expression; this fraternity, I say, is by no means, as the socialists believe, the principle of the perfectibility of society, the rule of its evolutions: it its only its goal and fruit. The point is not to know how, being brothers in spirit and of heart, we can live without making war and devouring each other: this is no easy question; but how, since we are brothers and sisters, we can become fraternal in our feelings; how our interests, instead of dividing us, can bring us together. Fraternity, solidarity, love, equality, etc., can only result from a reconciliation of interests, that is to say an organization of labor and a theory of exchange. Fraternity is the aim, not the starting point for the community, as with all

forms of association and government; and Plato, Cabet, and all those who begin with fraternity, solidarity and love, are taking the effect for the cause, the conclusion for the beginning; as in the proverb, they start building their house at the skylight[38].

This is not all; the danger of this moral solidarity basing itself in economic solidarity is a certain authoritarian tendency. The solidarists speak without cease about social duty, solidarist, corporatist, cooperativist duties, etc. New duties are called into existence. That is easy enough. But how about creating new virtues, and new energies?

Economic solidarity has often been presented under another name: that of the "general interest". But what does that mean? When we look closer, we see that the general interest is a fiction. We always find some particular interest at the head of what we call the general interest. It is true that the attempt has been made to identify personal selfishness and collective selfishness (Bentham). But nothing is more questionable than that project. John Stuart Mill, Bentham's disciple, clearly recognized this. As this identity is not a fact, but a simple *desideratum*, Mill suggests that it should be imposed on the social consciousness as a useful lie. By means of appropriate associations of ideas, the pedagogies and morals will factitiously establish in the minds of individuals an

---

[38] *System of Economical Contradictions*, Vol. II, p. 275

indissoluble link between the idea of personal interest and general interest. The efficacy of this expedient of duping the individual is dubious, to say the least; the individual will soon notice that the doctrine false. Against Mill's factitious associations he will practice the "dissociation of ideas" foreseen by Remy de Gourmont as an instrument of intellectual liberation. If this procedure were applied to the concept of the general interest, the latter would be likely to evaporate like the other abstract concepts which de Gourmont has analyzed in his fine book, *La culture des Idées.*

No matter how we look at it, the idea of solidarity appears as a vague concept or rather as a *psittacism.* Yet in economics, we need positive bases. We cannot take as a starting point some vague notion of solidarity or altruism. Thus, I believe that if socialism wishes to realize its destiny, it must courageously renounce, in economics, these vague principles of *solidarity* and *altruism.*

Why will men become socialists? Because they feel that the legitimate aspirations of their egoism are injured under present economic arrangements. We all view socialism a means of liberation and of flourishing for personal egoisms. The root of socialism is individualism, the protest of the individual against existing economic tyrannies; the desire to give more rein to the economic selfishness of each. Socialism is a doctrine of the expansion of life, and from the start life is selfishness. The English School was right to show that altruism is only selfishness, transformed and expanded.

Socialism should, essentially, be an economic technique for the more expansive flourishing of individual egoisms. As for altruism, as for the consideration of the general interest, as for solidarism, they will have their day; but as further additions, as an epiphenomenon of the implementation of selfish energies. Moreover, altruism and solidarity, having their origin in egoism, will also find their limits in it. Thus, socialism should be neither a religion, nor a mystique, nor an ethic. It should be and remain only an economic technique, a system of progressive economic experiments aiming to emancipate human egoisms. If socialism forgets this truth, if it aspires a basis in altruism alone or fraternity alone, which soon become authoritarian, it runs a great risk of perishing from a psychological error.

There is another threat to guard against. Namely, the idea that progress in intelligence will lead to intellectual solidarity. This notion is no less false that the other forms of solidarity that we have examined so far.

The tendency to denigrate the individual has appeared on the intellectual plane as it has elsewhere. Solitary thought — invention — has been depreciated in favor of collective thought — imitation — extolled under the eternal substantive of Solidarity. It is a characteristic of the Latin races, as Remy de Gourmont says, to spurn all new experiments, all intellectual and aesthetic originality. Regimented thought is preferred, along with conformist and decent meditation. A German writer, Madame Laura Marholm, has neatly analyzed this contemporary tendency:

> Intellectual cowardice is a universal trait. People do not dare to sever themselves from their surrounding culture. Nobody allows themselves any longer to think original thoughts. Original thought no longer dares to present itself except when supported by some group. It must have gathered many adherents before it will dare to show its face. It requires many voices before it dares to speak. We have in this an index of universal democratization, and a democratization that is yet in its infancy and which is characterized as a reaction against international Capital, which has thus far had at its disposition all the means of military and legislative defense. Nobody dares to lean on himself, alone. A thought which contravenes popular ideas almost never comes to light. The propagation of unpleasant ideas is circumvented and shackled by a thousand anonymous censures among which the official censure of the State has no longer but an effaced role.

> The first move that a man who feels favored by a novel idea, by a new thought, takes is to seek a social support, to form a group, a society, an association. That may be useful for

the inventor of an idea, but it is harmful to the idea itself. For this reason, most of the ideas in these days are as flat and shapeless as old coins. Every place in which the intervention of the individual is creative and fertile, instead we see the action of social circles, of chatterers, of smooth-talkers[39]...

The result of this tendency is that people no longer dare to be "selves" and to think by themselves. They think responsively and in the form of mottos.

Many seem to pose as an ideal the perfect uniformization of humanity. Gide says: "Man should tend to the unity of the human race." I regard the gradual uniformization of the economic conditions of humanity as both possible, desirable and likely. But an intellectual and aesthetic uniformization of humanity would be the death of culture. Instead, I hope for that future state which Tarde called the "ultimate individualism". To an external uniformization of humanity, there will be a corresponding growth of the diversity in internal consciousness, thanks to the greater complication and accumulated liberty in social relations. And then diversity will bloom, as the flower of the intellectual and aesthetic life.

Moral and social solidarity has also been posed as a desirable ideal by some writers. This solidarity must be understood a moral

---

[39] *Zur Psychologie der Frau*, p.219

uniformization, the moral dependence of the individual conscience on the collective conscience. Remy de Gourmont has highlighted the conflict that explodes here between the individual and the social consciousnesses, a conflict which is only one form of the fundamental conflict between the personal selfishness and the group's selfishness. He says:

> There is no doubt but that a man can derive, even from immorality, from insubordination to the canonized prejudices, great personal benefit, a great advantage for his integral development, but a collectivity of individuals who are too strong, and to interdependent, only constitutes a mediocre people. There, you find the social instinct enter into antagonism with the individual instinct and whole societies professing with one voice a morality which each of its intelligent members, followed by a huge part of the herd, reckons to be vain, outdated or tyrannical[40].

It is especially from the moral standpoint that the squashing of personal selfishness by the selfishness of the group is intolerable. It's no secret how the conniving of the *Esprit de corps*, the gregarious coalitions, enraged most of all against the superior individualities, solidarity for the sake of irresponsibility, and all these forms of diminished humanity. It is this solidarity that engenders all the coteries, camaraderies, warring schools of thought, societies for mutual admiration, etc. Faced with these excesses of

---

[40] Remy de Gourmont, *La Culture des Idées*, p. 83

shameful egoism, faced with the ambitions of so many people to control the behavior of others in the name of God knows what interests of the organization, of the group, etc., the best moral and social precept would be: "*Be selfish*. Pay attention to your own fate. That's hard enough to do. And be a little less worried about what will become of other people."

Solidarity favors those who scheme and plot, who flatter the powerful. It loathes the independent and the irritable. But the latter should get preference over the conspirators and the servile. For all that remains of our liberal force dwells in the irritable soul.

Let us conclude from this review of several forms of solidarity that it is impossible to set up collective selfishness as a dogma. One fails to see why selfishness should become sacrosanct by the simple fact of agglomeration. Let us also recall that these collective selfish egos remain on guard against each other, and that the law of the struggle for life, despite any optimistic affirmations to the contrary, implacably deploys its usual effects here as it does everywhere else.

It is the same with "perfect solidarity" as with "absolute justice", "absolute altruism", and "absolute monism". They are all abstract concepts, and impossible to translate into real terms. Every man has his own idiosyncratic notion of solidarity and justice, and his own way of judging right from wrong, by consequence of the interests of his coterie, class, etc. Remy de Gourmont said:

> After an idea has been dissociated, if it is then placed into circulation naked, during its voyage through the world it will pick up all sorts of parasitical passengers. Everywhere the first organism will disappear, entirely devoured by the egoistic colonies that develop on its back. A very amusing example of such deviations of ideas was recently given by the corporation of painters at the ceremony called of the "Triumph of the Republic". The workers carried a banner where their claims to social justice were summed up in this chant: "Down with the *ripolins!*" Now, the ripolin is a pre-painted wallpaper, ready for anyone to paste on wood paneling; there you can see the sincerity of their pledge, and its ingenuity. The ripolin represents injustice and oppression; it is the enemy, it is the devil. We all have our own ripolins and we color the abstract ideas as we please, which otherwise would be useless to us[41].

The ideal is sullied by contact with reality:

Perle avant de tomber et fange après sa chute[42].

And so it is absurd to want to realize these ideals which always flee from us with an eternal retreat,

---

[41] *La Culture des Idées*, p. 98

[42] Translator's note: "A pearl has fallen, now all I see is mire." From Victor Hugo's poem "Oh ! n'insultez jamais une femme qui tombe!"

to set as dogmas things that we can't even grasp. Absolute monism, absolute altruism, absolute justice, are all conceptual idols sitting enthroned in a metaphysical heaven, like the theses of the Kantian antinomies, of which, moreover they are only an aspect. They are like those "mothers" in the second Faust "which are enthroned in infinity, eternally alone, head encircled by images of life: active, but lifeless." According to Jules de Gaultier:

> In matters of happiness as in all other orders of conception, the metaphysical pretense of making things out of the Absolute defies the laws of our understanding, whose indefinite forms only create things that are relative. The secret sensibility of humanity rejects the insipidness of this perfect felicity. In harmony with the curiosity of the Intellect, whom all satisfaction attracts to a more anxious research, it recognizes itself to be insatiable. Goethe's Faust knew this law; he speculated on this form of human sensibility, duping Mephistopheles when he negotiated their pact on this condition, where he insists: "If you can seduce me to the point where I begin to find pleasure, if you can let me sleep in the heart of deepest enjoyments, let that be my last day! I offer you the bargain... If at that moment I say: "Slow down, you are so beautiful! then you can set the shackles on me straight away[43].
> .."

---

[43] Jules de Gaultier, *De Kant à Nietzsche*, p. 215

Faced with the bankruptcy of all the social dogmatisms *a priori* or *a posteriori*, only one party remains logical: that is, *anomie*, the autarky of the individual; it is individualism posed, not as a dogma (for this would be to resurrect a new Absolute), but as a tendency, a form of thought and action adapted to the fundamental law of our intellectual nature, which compels us to exist in a world of relativities.

There are, moreover, various ways to take Individualism. Each individual has his own way of affirming his own self. As Nietzsche wrote:

> Everyone feels freest where he *feels most alive*; hence, now in passion, now in duty, now in study, and now in caprice. A man unconsciously imagines that where he is strong, where he feels most alive, the element of his freedom must lie. He combines dependency and apathy, independence and vivacity as inseparable pairs... The strong man is also the free man; the vivid feeling of joy and sorrow, the high hopes, the keen desires, the powerful hatreds are the prerogative of the dominant and independent person, while the subject, the slave, lives in a state of dazed oppression[44].

Each type of human will have its own way of understanding individualism. In his fine study on *the forms of character*, Ribot has established that since the basis of every being is the will-to-

---

[44] Nietzsche, "The Wanderer and His Shadow", §9

live instead of its intelligence, the guiding principle for a division of human characteristics should be sought in the way they react to their will-to-live[45]. From this standpoint, he distinguishes the *sensitifs* from the *actifs*. Obviously the individualism of the *sensitifs* will not be the same as that of the *actifs*. The first will be an individualism of abstention and contemplation, the second a combative individualism. The first will nearly be an asceticism; the latter will be an attack, a conquest of life.

With regard to the extent of the sphere of social action, individualism can be conceived both broadly and narrowly. So we might speak of economic individualism, political individualism, and other individualisms: intellectual, aesthetic, religious, moral, social. Here a remark suggests itself on the subject of economic individualism as it has been professed by the liberal school. This economic philosophy has nothing individualistic about it aside from the name; for it ends as a veritable social dogmatism. With Spencer, for example, it is in the name of a dogmatic idol, *The Progress of the Species*, that the crushing of the economically weak is justified as both necessary and foreordained.

From the perspective of political organization, individualism can make room for two opposed forms: aristocratic individualism and democratic

---

[45] Théodule Ribot, *La Psychologie des Sentiments*

individualism. As I see it, aristocratic individualism is a contradictory individualism. For it only claims for a privileged few the integral blossoming of their self, and it becomes an oppressive doctrine for everyone else.

In the end, there is a final point on which individualism can allow for two opposite forms. This is the question of the intrinsic value and the probable destiny of human societies. Here two opposed conceptions come head to head: social optimism and social pessimism. — We may thus distinguish between two forms of individualism: optimist individualism and pessimist individualism.

The solution to the issue of social optimism and pessimism is a metaphysical problem, beyond the scope of our present work. Likewise, solving this problem would be to return to these social dogmatisms that we have already set aside.

The question at hand is a little different.

It consists in asking ourselves, all social dogmatism aside, what attitude will the individual have on the problem of *action*? I simply want to envision what links are possible between thought and action in the various hypotheses that suggest themselves to the individual who finds liberation from the social dogmatisms.

Since the instinct for knowledge has dissolved all the social dogmatisms, and even having taught the individual the inanity of every future dogmatism, will the individual not renounce action? Won't the instinct for knowledge, the critical instinct, be destructive of the vital instinct in the consciousness?

Gaultier[46] has done admirable work in explaining the role of the instinct for knowledge when facing the vital instinct. On one hand, the instinct for knowledge tends to deny life by constantly overturning the dogmatisms which the vital instinct of societies sets up for him to use. On the other hand, when these dogmatisms are overturned, the vital instinct summons other, more refined ones, by whose aid it may again subjugate the instinct for knowledge, until the latter revolts again and ends in fresh negations. This struggle between the instinct for life and the instinct for knowledge fills the history books. This antagonism between the vital instinct and the instinct for knowledge may be at the bottom of the antinomy between the individual and society. Society symbolizes the instinct for life. It seems to be a maniacal selfishness, a creator of useful myths, a frenzied illusionist, a deviser of ruses, to deceive individuals. Individual consciousness is the shelter — a precarious and fragile one — from the eternal enemy of the instinct for life: the instinct for knowledge. It is in the human *self* where the instinct for

[46] *De Kant à Nietzsche*, chapter 1

knowledge is incarnated. There it becomes aware of the omnipotence of its tyrant: the will-to-live. It is there, in the conscience of the individual, where the small liberating flame of intelligence flickers. From this small, luminous vantage point, lost in the night of Existence, the instinct for knowledge contemplates life and poses the question: What is it all worth?

We are led back to the issue posed above. From these two antagonistic instincts, the instincts for knowledge and for life, the first denying, the latter affirming life and action, which will the individual, liberated from dogmatism, follow?

With all the dogmatisms to one side, two hypotheses suggest themselves to the individual: the hypothesis of agnosticism and the hypothesis of absolute illusion.

Agnosticism refuses to answer the question of the value of social life in either direction. Between social optimism and social pessimism, it leaves the question open. — Does the agnostic hypothesis, against such excessive dogmatists as de Roberty, absolutely forbid the individual to take any action at all? Is it necessarily negative with respect to action? I don't believe so. In the absence of certainty, an act of faith will be enough to inspire the individual to take action. The individual can take Edmond Thiaudière's words as his motto: "Think like a skeptic, and act like a believer[47]."

---

[47] *La décevance du vrai*

To get beyond inaction and neutrality, life's pressures and the love of risk-taking, which Jean-Marie Guyau wrote about, are decisive.

But let us take on the other hypothesis: that of absolute illusion, of the absolute lie of life, where existence is nothing and human intelligence is a mere tool for filtering illusions, leaving only the more refined and delicate ones behind. — The solution seems simple and unilateral. That is, retire from all action and observe these illusions passively. At best, this supreme and aesthetic illusion called art becomes the individual's refuge. This is the mental attitude so well described by Jules de Gaultier.

> By the production of works of art, the intelligence announces that it has retired from the scene where it once acted under the sway of illusion, and that it now sits as a spectator on the banks of the future, on the shore of the river while the ships, full of masks and values invented by the folly of Maya, flow on downstream amid all of life's noisiness.

This attitude seems to the only logical one. But let us not forget that humanity comes in two classes, the passive and the active. — Passive natures, enlightened by the instinct for knowledge, will end up in the Hinduistic state, as I have just mentioned. But it is not so with active natures. For them the voice of life, of action, will always ring louder than the voice of disillusionment.

In them, despite everything, the will-to-live, that brutal and eternal victor, will triumph. These natures are destined for action. For them, *Faust*'s words are true: "In the beginning was action." And action is also at the end. In them it is the final *élan*, the final cry of life.

Thus, the active man will act, even if he feels, if he knows that he lives within eternal illusion. He will be intoxicated by the spectacle of life; possessed by the shadows, he will leap after illusions and mirages. The active man, faced with the moving décor of life, is like those attending a play who are so taken in by the illusion that they try to intervene in the show, like that theater-goer who is said to have screamed "Stop! she's innocent!" at Othello as he killed Desdemona.

Those in whom the will-to-live and the will-to-power triumph will always project on the world the mirage of energy that brims over in them. — At first contact with their powerful wills, pale Maya will seem to become animate, as the statue of Galatea once did. Having felt Maya shudder under their embrace, these energetic ones are left with the most intoxicating sensation, which makes them shiver with joy as they barrel along through the phenomenon called Life.

ANARCHISM AND INDIVIDUALISM

The terms "anarchism" and "individualism" are often used interchangeably. Many thinkers who are, moreover, vastly different from each other, are called, more or less at random, either anarchists or individualists. Thus we speak carelessly of Stirnerite anarchism or Individualism, of Nietzschean anarchism or individualism, of Barrèsian anarchism or individualism[48], etc. And yet, in other cases this identification of the two terms is not seen as possible. Some often refer to Proudhonian anarchism, Marxist anarchism, Syndicalist anarchism; but never to Proudhonian, Marxist, or syndicalist individualism. We can talk about Christian or Tolstoyan anarchism, but not Christian or Tolstoyan individualism.

On other occasions, both terms have been combined into a single epithet: *Anarchist*

---

[48] To tell the truth, the social philosophy of Stirner, that of Nietzsche and that of Maurice Barrès (in *Un homme libre* and in *l'Ennemi des lois*) should rather, as we will see after establishing certain distinctions, deserve the label of individualism rather than anarchism

Individualism. Victor Basch uses this rubric to designate a social philosophy which he distinguishes from anarchism properly speaking, whose leading representatives are, for him, people like Goethe, Byron, Von Humboldt, Schleiermacher, Carlyle, Emerson, Kierkegaard, Renan, Ibsen, Stirner, Nietzsche[49]. This philosophy can be summarized as the worship of great men and the apotheosis of genius. As a label suited to that doctrine, the expression "anarchist individualism" seems debatable to me. The label "anarchist", taken etymologically, seems hardly applicable to thinkers in the lineage of Goethe, Carlyle, and Nietzsche, whose philosophy appears rather to be dominated by ideas of both hierarchical organization and the harmonious stratification of values. On the other hand, the epithet "individualist" may not be applied with equal propriety to all those who named above. While it may seem suitable for Stirner's Egotist, Nihilist, and anti-Idealist revolt, it is hard to see how it would apply to the Hegelian, Optimist, and Idealist philosophy of someone like Carlyle, who clearly subordinates the individual to the Idea.

---

[49] See Basch, *L'individualisme anarchiste, Max Stirner* (F. Alcan), p. 276

So there is some confusion on the use of these two terms, anarchism and individualism, as well as with regard to the ideas and feelings indicated by these terms. In this essay I will attempt to clarify the notion of individualism and determine what its psychological and sociological content is, by distinguishing it from anarchism[50].

* * *

Let us begin with a clear distinction: that is, between a social system and a simple intellectual or sentimental attitude. It seems that the differences between anarchism and individualism start there. Anarchism, in no matter which of its formulations, is essentially a social system: an economic, political and social doctrine, which seeks to realize a certain ideal. Even Bakunin's amorphism, which is defined by the absence of every definite social form, remains a particular social system in the final analysis. On the other hand, individualism seems to be a mental state, a feeling of life, a certain

---

[50] I have attempted to defend, in my book *Combat pour l'Individu*, a certain individualism which many of my critics have called an intellectual anarchism. The label "anarchist" causes me no alarm. But, for the sake of clarity in my ideas, I think it only right to keep the two expressions, anarchism and individualism, separate.

intellectual and sentimental attitude of the individual vis-à-vis his society.

I am aware that sociological terminology presents a certain individualism which we call *legal individualism*. This individualism proclaims the functional identity of human individualities, and their consequential equality before the law. In this there is a well-defined juridical and political doctrine and not a simple mental attitude. But it is all too plain that this doctrine has nothing individualist about it except its name. In effect, it focuses exclusively on what all humans share in common; by design it neglects that which is diverse, singular, and properly individual in them; instead, it regards these as a source of disorder and evil. It is clear that this doctrine is more a form of humanism or socialism than a veritable individualism.

What, then, is individualism? Understood in the subjective and psychological sense, which I will explain further, individualism is a spirit of antisocial revolt. This, for the individual, is the feeling of a pressure, to some extent a painful one, arising from life in society; at the same time, it is a wish to rebel against the ambient social determinism and to remove one's personality from it.

That a struggle exists between the individual and his social milieu cannot be denied. It is axiomatic of sociology is that society is something more than a sum of unities. By the fact of the reconciliation of these unities, the common and similar parts tend to mutually reinforce each other, and crush the parts that are not held in common. A certain notion of an external social order, which is superior to individuals, takes shape and imposes itself on them. It is incarnated in the rules, customs, disciplines and laws, in the totality of a social organization, which acts incessantly upon the individual. On the other hand, in every individual (of course to a degree that varies with the individual in question), differences in sensibility, intelligence, and willpower emerge and resist the leveling that inevitably comes with social life; consequently, certain instincts of independence, enjoyment, and power also emerge, seeking room to blossom, which look on social norms as so many obstacles. Those sociologists and moralists who speak on behalf of the interests of society can call such tendencies "vagabond", inconsequential, irrational, and dangerous if they like; but they do exist all the same. It is futile for society to brutally and hypocritically try to suppress them; it is vain for society to multiply its efforts at intimidation, vexation and elimination against the independent man and the rebel; it is futile to try to convince the individual of his own weakness and nothingness, by the mouths of its moralists; the feeling of the self — the self, which society hates — yet remains indestructible in certain souls and there it invincibly provokes the individualist revolt.

* * *

Two phases can be distinguished in the evolution of the individualist sentiment. First, the individual becomes aware of the social determinism that weighs him down. But at the same time he gets the sense that he himself constitutes a force in the midst of all this determinism. A very weak force, if you please, but one that is essentially capable, in spite of everything, of struggle, and perhaps of victory. In any case, he refuses to submit without trying his strength against society, and he takes up his struggle against it, counting on his own forces, his suppleness, and if pressed, his lack of scruples. Such is the history of the great ambitious men, the merciless power-seekers. In

Stendhal's novel *The Red and the Black*, Julian Sorel represents this archetype in literature. Cardinal de Retz, Napoleon, and Benjamin Constant represent it in the real world, with varying degrees of energy, absence of scruples and successful outcomes.

No matter which qualities are deployed by the strong individuality in his struggle for independence and power, it is rare for it to come off victorious in this unequal match. Society is too strong; it envelops us with too solid a network of obligations for us to defeat it for long. The romantic theme of the epic combat between the strong individuality and society is never without a leitmotiv of discouragement and despair; it invariably ends with an admission of defeat. As Vigny said:

> God set Earth amid the air, and man amid destiny. Destiny envelops him and carries him towards the eternally hidden goal. The common man is simply carried along; the great characters are those who struggle against it. There are few who have fought it all their lives; when they give in to the current, these swimmers drown. Thus Bonaparte was weakened in Russia, then he became ill and

struggled no further: destiny swallowed him up. Cato was his own master to the end[51].

A sense of powerless revolt against the social conditions that fate had cast him into, full of the de Couaen's Romantic imprecations. De Camors's will reeks of the final lassitude of a defeated man. The king's sons in Gobineau's novel *Les Pléiades* declare war on society, but they cave in to their sense that the enemy is too powerful, fearing that the imbecile mob will crush them. Again, Vigny:

> The desert, alas! It is you, egalitarian democracy, it is you, who buried and made everything grow pale beneath heaps of minute grains of sand. Your ponderous leveling has buried and razed everything. The valleys and hills are forever displaced, and courageous men only appear from time to time; they burst upwards like a waterspout, take ten steps toward the sun, then fall down pulverized, and then we lost sight of everything but the sinister, flat sand[52].

---

[51] Vigny, *Journal d'un poète*
[52] Vigny, *Journal d'un poète*, p. 262

Benjamin Constant recognized the tyrannical omnipotence of society over the individual, both in feelings and in behavior. "Even the most passionate feelings cannot wage war on the order of things. Society is too powerful, it is reproduced under too many forms, it mixes too much bitterness into all unsanctioned love[53]..."

The feeling which results for the strong individualities is that of a hopeless disproportion between their aspirations and their destiny. Trapped between opposing fates, they writhe in weakness and exasperation. Statements to this effect abound in Vigny:

> To be honest, there are only two kinds of men: those who *have* and those who *earn*... As for me, although I was born to the first of these classes, I have had to live like the second, and the feeling of this destiny that should not have been mine repulsed me deeply[54].

People like Heine present the same spectacle of painful non-adaptation, this nomadism and rootlessness of a superior individuality which is torn between the existing social influences,

---

[53] Benjamin Constant, *Adolphe*, p. 202
[54] Vigny, *Journal d'un poète*, p. 236

between antagonistic ideals and parties, refusing to be tied down anywhere. "What the world pursues and aspires to nowadays," wrote Heine in 1848, "has become completely foreign to my heart; I bow to destiny, I am too weak to resist it."

Aside from these revolts in the grand style, there are others on a smaller scale. These are the everyday malcontents who, incapable of single-handedly confronting a society they deem oppressive, combine forces with other individuals who feel equally outraged. These malcontents create small societies, at odds with the surrounding one. The same thing occurs in all revolutionary parties. Although small in their beginnings, they tend to enlarge and transform society in their own image. Understood in this way, the spirit of revolt is very much a social solvent; but it is also the seed of a new society. It plays an important historical role, and represents the spirit of change and progress.

But here again, individual efforts to shake off the existing servitudes end in deception. One defeated tyranny is replaced by another. The victorious minority transforms itself into a tyrannical majority. This is the vicious cycle of all politics. Progress, in the sense of the enfranchisement of the individual, is never more than an illusion. In reality, all that ever occurs is the transfer of influences and servitudes. Under the pressure of a revolutionary minority, the collective ideals and feelings attach to other objects and are incarnated in a new ideal. But, as things that are collectivized and shared by large numbers, these ideas and feelings immediately tend to become imperatives. Crystallized as dogmas and norms, they become new authorities who refuse to allow the same contradictions that destroyed their predecessors. The logical conclusion of this vicious circle of history seems to be Vigny's solution: namely, political indifference: "How little it matters to us which troop marches onto the stage of Power[55]."

* * *

We now come to the second phase of individualism. The first was the courageous and confident revolt of the individual who flattered himself that he was able to dominate society and refashion it according to whim. The second is the feeling of the futility of all effort. This is a forced resignation in the face of social constraints and

[55] Vigny, *Journal d'un poète*

inevitabilities, which, in spite of all is mixed with an irreducible hostility. Individualism is the eternal loser, but it can never be tamed. This is the spirit of revolt, so admirably symbolized by Leconte de Lisle in his Caïn and his Satan.

From the start, Cain throws his cry of revolt in God's face:

Why should we roam forever in the
sacred shadow,
Panting like a timber wolf until morning
comes?
To the clarity of distant Paradise;
Why do you always offer your parched
lips?
Bow your head, slave, and suffer your
destiny, your fate.

Go back to nothingness, earthworm!
What matters your useless revolt to He
who can do anything?
The fire laughs at the water that
murmurs and boils;
The wind does not hearken to the protest
of the dry leaf.
Pray and prostrate yourself. — I shall
remain standing!

May the coward crawl under the
conqueror's feet.
Glorify shame, worship torment,
And pay for your repose with
degradation;
Jehovah can bless their filth and shame;
The flattering fear and the hatred that
tells lies.

I shall remain standing!
And from evening till dawn;
And from dawn to the night,
I will never keep mute;
The tireless cry of a desperate heart!
The thirst for justice, O Cherub, devours
me.
Crush me down, or I will never bow!

In the *Tristesse du Diable*, the poet expresses the wrestler's discouragement:

The monotonous days, like a horrible
rain;
Pile up, without being filled, in my
eternity;

*Power, pride, despair, everything is only
vanity;
And the fury weighs on me and the
struggle wears me down.*

*As with love, hatred has lied to me!
I drank all the sea of infertile tears.
Fall, crush me, thunder, heaps of worlds;
May I be engulfed in the sacred sun!*

*And the happy cowards, and the
suffering races;
By bright space which has neither bottom
nor end;
Will hear a voice saying: Satan is dead!
And that will be your end,
You who took six days to create!*

Let's come down to Earth from all that symbolism. In Earthly terms, individualism is the feeling of a profound, irreducible antinomy between the individual and society. The individualist is he who, by virtue of his temperament, is predisposed to a particularly lively sense of the ineluctable disharmonies between his intimate being and his social milieu. At the same time this man has been given some decisive occasion to see this disharmony in action. In him, either by some act of violence or after a succession of experiences, society shows itself to him as a perpetual producer of constraint, humiliation, and misery, a continually renewed creation of human suffering. In the name of his own experience and his personal sensation of life, the individualist thinks he has a right to consider every ideal of a future society, in which a desired harmony would be established between the individual and society, as utopian. Far from reducing its evils, the development of civilization only intensifies them by making the individual's life more complicated, more laborious, and more difficult with the thousand wheels of the social mechanism which become ever more tyrannical. Science itself, by intensifying the individual's awareness of his socially-imposed conditions of life, ends by darkening his intellectual and moral horizons. *Qui auget scientiam auget et dolorem*[56].

It's well known that individualism is essentially a social pessimism. In its more moderate form, it allows that, if life in society is not absolutely evil and completely destructive to individuality, it is at minimum a restrictive and oppressive condition for the individual: a compulsory move

---

[56] Translator's note: "He who increases his knowledge increases his sorrows." - Seneca

in the game of life, a necessary evil, and a last resort.

The individualists who respond to this signal are only a small, morose group whose language is rebellious, resigned, and desperate, in stark contrast to the futurist fanfares heard from the direction of every optimistic sociologist. Vigny, for example: "The social order is always bad. Occasionally it becomes tolerable, but no more. Between the bad and the tolerable, the dispute is not worth a single drop of blood[57]". Or Schopenhauer, reflecting on social life as the absolute efflorescence of human wickedness and misery. Or Stirner, with his intellectual and moral solipsism, forever on his guard against the tricks of social idealism, and against the intellectual and moral crystallization which every organized society brings to bear against the individual. Or, sometimes, Amiel with his painful stoicism which sees society as a limitation and an encumbrance for his free, spiritual nature. Or Henry David Thoreau, that outrageous Emersonian, the "bachelor of nature," scrupulously avoiding all normal paths of human activity and becoming a "stroller," enamored with independence and dreams, "whose every

---

[57] Vigny, *Journal d'un poète*

instant will always be filled with truer work than what normally employed men can experience during their whole life." Or Challemel-Lacour with his pessimistic conception of society and progress. Or, perhaps at certain times also, Gabriel Tarde, purveyor of an individualism tinged by misanthropy, which he expresses in one of his books:

> It is possible that the river of imitation has its banks and that, by the very effect of its excessive deployment, the need for sociability diminishes or rather is altered and transformed into a kind of generalized misanthropy, which, moreover, is quite compatible with a modest commercial circulation and a certain degree of industrial exchange, activities reduced to the strictly necessary, but above all very well suited to reinforce in each of us the distinctive traits of our internal individuality[58].

Even with those who, like Maurice Barrès, are disgusted, either due to dilettantism and artistic obligations, or the accents of bitter rebellion or discouraged pessimism, with such men individualism remains a feeling of "the impossibility of reconciling the 'particular ego'

---

[58] Tarde, *Les Lois de l'imitation*

and the 'general ego'[59]". This is a will to liberate the first 'ego', to cultivate that which is most special, most driven and sought after, in detail and depth. As Barrès says:

> The individualist is he who, through the pride of his true ego, which he fails to liberate, then ceaselessly murders, disfigures and denies everything he has in common with ordinary men... The dignity of the men of our race is exclusively attached to certain stirrings, which the world neither knows nor perceives, which we must cultivate in ourselves.

With everyone, individualism is an attitude of sensibility that goes on from hostility and suspicion to indifference and disdain vis-à-vis organized society where we are constrained to live, regarding its uniformizing rules, its monotonous repetitions and its subjugating constraints. This is a desire of his to escape and to retreat into himself, *phuguê monou pros monon*[60]. It is over all the profound feeling of the "unicity of the self" of what the self retains of itself, which is incompressible and impervious to all social influences. It is, as Tarde says, the

---

[59] M. Barrès, *Un Homme libre*
[60] Translator's note: "The passing from the solitary to the solitary"

feeling of the "profound and fugitive singularity of persons, of their way of being, of thinking, feeling, which only occurs once and only for an instant[61]."

* * *

Do I really need to point out how much this attitude differs from anarchism?

Doubtless, in one sense, anarchism emanates from individualism[62]. It is, in effect, the antisocial revolt of a minority who feels oppressed or disadvantaged by the current order of things. But anarchism only represents the first stage of individualism: the stage of faith and hope, of courageous action confident of success. Individualism in its second phase converts, as we have seen, into social pessimism.

The passage from confidence to desperation, from optimism to pessimism is here, in large part, a function of psychological temperament. There are delicate souls who crumple at the least

---

[61] Tarde, *Les Lois de l'imitation*, sub fine

[62] On this point Nietzsche said: "Anarchism is only a means of individualist agitation" (*Will to Power*, Section 337)

contact with social realities and are consequently quick to lose their illusions, I mean people like Vigny or Heine. Souls like these might be classified as the psychological type that has been called the *sensitifs*. In them the feeling of social control, in its compressive impact on the individual, is particularly disturbing and crushing. But there are other souls who resist multiple failures, remaining ignorant even of experience's hardest lessons, and unshakable in their faith. These souls belong to the *actif* type. Such are the apostles of anarchism: Bakunin, Kropotkin, Reclus. Maybe their imperturbable confidence in their ideal clings to a lesser intellectual and emotional acuity. The reasons for doubt and discouragement do not strike them so vividly as to tarnish the abstract ideal that they have fashioned or lead them to the final and logical stage of individualism: social pessimism.

Whatever the truth may be, that the anarchist philosophy is an optimistic one is not in question. This optimism, often a simplistic and naive one, is diffused in their volumes bound with oxblood covers, which form domestic libraries of the *propagandists by the deed!* The shadow of Rousseau's optimism broods over all this literature. The anarchist optimism consists in believing that the social disharmonies, that the antinomies in the present state of affairs between the individual and society are not essential, but accidental and temporary; that they one day will be resolved, making way for an era of harmony.

Anarchism hinges on two principles which seem complementary, but which are in fact contradictory at bottom. The first is the properly idealist or libertarian principle formulated by Wilhelm von Humboldt and chosen by John Stuart Mill as the epigraph for his *Essay on Liberty*: "The great principle is the essential and absolute importance of human development in its richest diversity." The other is the humanist or altruist principle which is translated on the economic plane by anarchist communism. — That the individualist principle and the humanist principle negate each other, has been proven by both logic and the facts. Either the individualist principle has no meaning, or it is a defense of all the diversity and inequality of the individuals concerned, in favor of traits which differentiate them, separate them, and on occasion set them against each other. Humanism, on the other hand, envisions the assimilation of the human species. Its ideal is, according to Gide's expression, is to make the expression, *nos semblables*[63] a reality. In fact, the mutual antagonism of these two principles has been affirmed in the writings of the more astute anarchist theoreticians; and this logical and necessary antagonism will not fail to lead to the disintegration of anarchism as a political and social doctrine[64].

Whatever the truth may be, and whatever obstacles may meet he who would reconcile the individualist principle and the humanist principle, these two rival and inimical principles are at least agreed in their manifest optimism. Humboldt's principle is optimistic in that it implicitly affirms the original goodness of human nature and the legitimacy of its free flourishing. It is opposed to the Christian condemnation of our natural instincts, and we conceive the reservations that Dupont-White, the translator of the *Essay on Liberty*, thought he should make on the spiritualist and Christian point of view (condemnation of the flesh) as

---

[63] Translator's note: In French, a dual meaning could be derived: both *our fellows* and *those who are like us*

[64] I allude here to a recent and very interesting debate between two theoreticians of anarchism, Malato and Janvion, in the journal *l'Ennemi du Peuple* (1903) and to a series of articles entitled *Individualisme et Humanisme*, by Janvion in the same journal. The conflict between individualism and humanism becomes quite heated in this debate, in which Janvion, the opponent of humanism, seems by far to bring the better arguments.

concerning this principle[65]. The humanist principle is no less optimistic. In effect, humanism is nothing other than the divinization of man in his general qualities, of the human species and consequently of human society. It's plain to see that if anarchism is optimistic relative to the individual, it is even more so relative to society. Anarchism presupposes that individual liberties, freed unto themselves, will harmonize naturally, and will spontaneously realize the anarchist ideal of the free society.

---

[65] "Oh, no," says Dupont-White, "I cannot accept this dogma! It is not right to ask men to reveal themselves as they are, to put everything on display. If our nature were all the same in the sense of being purely spiritual, we might yet indulge it and encourage a free expression of its full breadth: man's wandering astray would be no occasion for alarm... but when a being who bears such different impulses within his bosom, which are so much at odds, is it not quite a risky venture to agree to the development of 'all his nature in its richest diversity?' But you might repeat Fourier to me, saying that 'the passions come from God while duty comes from man.' This is at best too complacent in the face of widely varying inclinations, some of them quite perverse, which persist so strongly with we superior apes." The conclusion is close to Brunetière's: "Do refrain from provoking a being who is so well formed and so well conditioned to blossoming beyond all proportion. Should he wish to cultivate himself and manifest himself in certain respects, so be it: but above all, let him restrict himself, let him reduce himself, let him efface himself, this ideal suits him best. Besides, there is no doubt here: we only enter into society in order to see some benefit from mutual constraint, and, I would almost say, universal mutilation." (Dupont-White, "préface a *l'Essai sur la Liberté*" by John Stuart Mill)

With respect to these two opposed perspectives, the Christian and the anarchist ones, what is the attitude of individualism?

Individualism, a realist philosophy that come from lived experience and immediate sensation, rejects both of these metaphysics equally: the former, the Christian metaphysics, which affirms *a priori* an original perversity; the other, the rationalistic and Rousseavian metaphysics, which affirms no less *a priori* the original and essential goodness of our nature. — Individualism faces the facts. And these reveal in the human being of a bundle of instincts warring against each other, and in human society, a grouping of individuals who also struggle against each other. By the facts of the conditions of his existence, the human being is subject to the law of struggle: an internal struggle between his own instincts, an external struggle with his fellows. If, to recognize the permanent and universal character of egoism and struggle in human existence, is being pessimistic, then I concede that individualism is pessimistic. But we must quickly add that the pessimism of individualism, the pessimism of facts, in a sense, the experiential pessimism, as a pessimism *a posteriori*, is wholly different from the theological pessimism which pronounces *a priori*, in the name of Dogma, its condemnation of human nature.

On the other hand, individualism is no less clearly distinguishable from anarchism. If, like anarchism, it allows von Humboldt's principle as an expression of the normal and necessary tendency of our nature in full bloom, it also recognizes that this tendency is doomed to perpetual frustration, given the internal and external disharmonies of our nature[66]. In other terms, it considers the harmonious development of the individual and society as a utopian ideal. — As pessimistic as it is relative to the individual, individualism is even more so relative to society: Man is by nature a disharmonious being, by reason of the internal struggle of his instincts. But this disharmony is compounded in the state of society, which, by a painful paradox, compresses our instincts at the same time that it exasperates them. In effect, when the individual wills-to-life join together, they form themselves

---

[66] Metchnikoff, despite his optimism, recognizes the disharmonies of human nature in moral and social life to their full extent. It is also true that he seems to expect science to make progress in attenuating these disharmonies. See E. Metchnikoff, *Études sur la nature humaine, Essai de philosophie optimiste*, pp. 137ff

into a collective will-to-live which immediately starts to oppress the individual will-to-live and powerfully opposes their expansion. Thus, the state of society pushes the disharmonies of our nature to their limits; it exasperates them and highlights them most dreadfully. Thus, as Schopenhauer thought, society truly represents the human will-to-live in its apex of desire, struggle, dissatisfaction, and suffering.

* * *

From this first opposition between anarchism and individualism, others can also be derived.

Anarchism believes in Progress. Individualism is a mental attitude that might be called ahistorical. It denies the future and progress. It see the human will-to-live in an eternal present. Like Schopenhauer, with whom he often agrees, Stirner thought ahistorically. He likewise believed that the anticipation of some new and marvelous thing to come, is illusory. Every social form, when it becomes concretized, crushes the individual. For Stirner, there is no utopian tomorrow, no "paradise at the end of our days"; there is only the egoistic today.

Stirner's attitude toward society is the same as Schopenhauer's: the negation of life remains entirely metaphysical, and, as it were, entirely spiritual (don't forget that Schopenhauer condemns suicide, which would constitute its material and tangible negation). Similarly, Stirner's rebellion against society is entirely mental, entirely internal, entirely of the intention and the internal will. It is not, as with someone like Bakunin, a call to pandestruction. It is, relative to society, a simple act of defiance and passive hostility, a combination of indifference and spiteful resignation. It is about encouraging the individual to struggle against society; society will always win. It must be obeyed, then, — obey it like a dog would. But Stirner, while running about obediently, yet retains, by way of consolation, a great deal of intellectual contempt for it. This is nearly Vigny's attitude vis-à-vis nature and society. "A peaceable despair, with neither fits of anger nor curses to heaven, is wisdom itself[67]." And again: "Silence is the best critique of life."

Anarchism is an exasperated and insane form of idealism. Individualism is summed up by a trait that Schopenhauer and Stirner have in common:

[67] Vigny, *Journal d'un poète*

their merciless realism. It ended in what a German writer calls a fundamental "de-idealization" (*Entidealisierung*)[68] of life and society. "An ideal is only a peg", said Stirner. — From this perspective, Stirner is the most authentic representative of individualism. His frosty words seize your soul with a shudder that is quite removed from Nietzsche's fiery, radiant language. Nietzsche remains an impenitent, imperious, and violent idealist. He idealizes the superior humanity. Stirner represents the most complete de-idealization of nature and life, the most radical philosophy of disillusionment since the book of Ecclesiastes.

While it is pessimistic beyond measure and without hesitation, individualism is also absolutely antisocial, as opposed to anarchism, which is only relatively so (that is, relative to the present form of society).

Anarchism certainly recognizes the existence of an antinomy between the individual and the State, an antinomy that it seeks to resolve by suppressing the State; but it can see no

---

[68] The expression in from J. Volkelt's book *A. Schopenhauer, seine Persönlichkeit, seine Lehre, sein Glaube*, p. 47

fundamental, irreducible antinomy between the individual and society. While hurling curses against the State, anarchism absolves and almost divinizes society. For it, society represents a spontaneous growth (Spencer), while the State is an artificial and authoritarian organization[69]. However, for the individualist, society is just as tyrannical, if not more so, than the State. Society is, in effect, nothing other than the ensemble of every sort of social bond (opinion, morals, customs, propriety, mutual surveillance, more or less discreet spying on each other's behavior, moral approbation, and reproof, etc). Thus understood, society comprises a tight web of tyrannies both major and minor, which are demanding, inexorable, unceasing, harassing and pitiless, which reach into the details of individual lives far more profoundly and continually than any statist constraint could ever do. In addition, upon close examination one finds that statist tyranny and the tyranny of custom grow out of the same root: the collective interest of a caste or a class which desires to establish or maintain its domination and prestige. Opinion and custom are partially a residue from the old, vanishing caste disciplines, and in part the germ of new social discipline that

---

[69] See also, on this point, Bakunin, *Federalisme, socialisme, et antitheologisme*, pp. 285ff

are bringing with them a new directing class that is in the process of formation. This is why there is only a difference of degree between the constraints of the State and those of opinion and custom. They have, at bottom, the same goal: to maintain a particular moral conformity that the group finds useful, and same methods: the vexation and elimination of all independent and refractory spirits. The only difference is that the more diffuse sanctions (opinion and custom) are more hypocritical than the others.

Proudhon was right to say that the State is only the mirror of society. It is only tyrannical when society is tyrannical. The government, as Tolstoy pointed out, is an assembly of people who exploit others and favor the wicked and cheats in particular. If this is the practice of the government, it is also that of society. These two terms are harmonious: State and society. The first has the same value as the second. The gregarious spirit or the spirit of society is no less oppressive for the individual than the statist spirit or the priestly spirit, which are only maintained thanks to it and by its action. But how odd! When it comes to the relations of society and the State, even Stirner seems to share Spencer's and Bakunin's error. He protests against State intervention in the acts of the individual, but not against that of society:

Before the individual, the State is surrounded by an aura of sanctity; for example it makes a law about duels. Two men who agree to risk their lives in order to resolve an affair (whatever it may be) cannot carry out their agreement because the State would forbid it; they will be exposed to prosecution and some form of punishment. What of their liberty and free will? Things are different where, as in North America, society resolves to make the duelists suffer certain unpleasant *consequences* of their act, and, for example, withdraw from them the credit which they previously enjoyed. To refuse credit is a private affair, and if it pleases a society to retract it from some reason or another, he who suffers this cannot complain of an attack on their liberty: society has only made use of its own. The society of which we speak leaves the individual perfectly free to be exposed to fatal or disagreeable consequences that their way of acting will bring, leaving the liberty of their will full and entire. The State does precisely the opposite: it denies all legitimacy to the will of the individual and does not recognize as legitimate any will but its own, the law of the State[70].

---

[70] Stirner, *The Ego and His Own*, "My Intercourse"

What a strange argument. The law does not strike me. How then am I more free if society boycotts me? Arguments like this would legitimate every assault by public opinion, under the influence of moral bigotry, against the individual. It is on such reasoning that the legend of individual liberty in the Anglo-Saxon countries is fabricated[71]. Stirner himself has a vivid sense of the weakness of this argument, and a little further on he draws his famous distinction between *society* and *association*[72]. In the former, the individual is taken as a means; in the latter, he takes himself as an end and treats the association as a means to personal power and enjoyment:

> You bring to association all your power, all your wealth, and there you make yourself *count*. In society, you and your activity *were utilized*. In the former, you live as an egoist;

[71] What provides even more support for placing the State and society on a level, and the fact that liberalism in the former is little different from that of the latter, is the recent measure taken by the American State against the Russian writer Gorky in the well-known circumstances. — Such a measure, which fortunately would seem impossible and absurd in France, is only possible down there thanks to a certain state of public opinion.

[72] Translator's note: English translations of Stirner prefer the word "union" for Stirner's *verein*

in the second, you live as a man, that is, religiously: you labor there in the Lord's vineyard. You owe to society all that you have, you are in its debt and you are possessed by social duties; while in association, you owe nothing to it; it serves you, and you leave it without scruple when you cease to derive any advantage from it... If society is more than you, you will bring it face to face with yourself, you will make it your servant; association is your tool, your weapon, it sharpens and multiplies your natural strength. Association only exists for your sake, and by you, while society on the contrary claims you as its property and may exist without you. In brief, society is sacred and association is *your property*, society uses you, while you use association[73].

An empty distinction, if there ever was one! Where exactly is the line between a society and an association? Does association not quickly tend, as Stirner himself avows, to crystallize immediately into society?

No matter how we take it, anarchism finds itself in the impossible position of trying to reconcile two antinomical terms: society and individual

---

[73] Max Stirner, *The Ego and His Own*, "My Intercourse"

liberty. The "free society" it yearns for is a contradiction in terms. This is nothing but *wooden iron*, a baton with no bottom. Speaking of anarchists, Nietzsche wrote: "one already reads their watchword of the future: *free society*, on all tables and walls. — A free society, indeed! But what material, sirs, will you use to build it? — Wooden iron[74]?" ... Individualism is more clear and more frank than anarchism is. It places the State, society, and association the same level; it lines them all up and throws them overboard as far it can. As Vigny says, "Every association has the same flaws as monasteries."

As antisocial as it is, individualism is also gleefully immoralistic. But this is not true in an absolute sense. For Vigny, pessimistic individualism can be reconciled with an elevated, severe and pure moral stoicism. But even with Vigny, an immoralistic element is always there: a tendency to de-idealize society, to decouple and set the terms "society" and "morality" against each other, and to see society as the necessary mother of cowardice, stupidity, and hypocrisy. "*Cinq-Mars, Stello, Servitude et Grandeur militaires* are each cantos in a sort of epic poem on the subject of disillusionment; but it is only

[74] Nietzsche, *The Gay Science*, Section 356

the social and false things that I will ruin and trample underfoot as the illusions that they are; I will raise upon these debris, on this dust, the holy beauty of enthusiasm, of love, of honor[75]..." It goes without saying that for Stirner and Stendhal, individualism is immoralistic, without scruple or reservation. — Anarchism is imbued with a rather vulgar moralism. Anarchist morality, while lacking both obligations and sanctions, is still a morality. It is, at bottom, the Christian morality, stripped of its pessimistic shell. The anarchist assumes that the virtues necessary for social harmony will flourish of their own accord. Inimical to coercion, the doctrine even grants the lazy the right to take from the general storehouse as he pleases. But the anarchist is persuaded that, in the future city, the lazy will be rare or even nonexistent.

* * *

Optimistic and idealistic, imbued with humanism and moralism, anarchism is a social dogmatism. It is a "cause", in Stirner's sense of that term. A "cause" is one thing; a simple attitude of the individual soul is another. A cause implies a communal adherence to an idea, a

[75] Vigny, *Journal d'un poète*, p. 17

shared belief and a shared devotion to this belief. This, individualism is not. Individualism is anti-dogmatic and has little inclination for proselytism. It gladly takes Stirner's words as its motto: "I have taken nothing as my cause." The veritable individualist does not seek to communicate his own sensation of life and society. What good would that do? *Omne individuum ineffabile*[76]. Persuaded of the diversity of temperaments and the uselessness of a single rule, he gladly echoes Henry David Thoreau:

> I would not have any one adopt my mode of living on any account; for, beside that before he has fairly learned it I may have found out another for myself, I desire that there may be as many different persons in the world as possible; but I would have each one be very careful to find out and pursue *his own way*, and not his father's or his mother's or his neighbor's instead[77].

The individualist knows that some temperaments find individualism repulsive, and that it would be ridiculous to try and win them over to his side. For a thinker enamored of

---

[76] Translator's note: Latin, "Every individual is ineffable"
[77] Translator's note: Thoreau, *Walden*, chapter 1-E

solitude and independence, a deep thinker, like Vigny a pure adept of the inner life, the social life and its agitations look artificial, rigged, deprived of any sincere or deeply held feelings. And, conversely, those who by temperament feel a driving need for social life and activity, who leap with both feet into the melee, who are enthused about political and social matters, who accept the virtue of certain leagues and groupings, who ceaselessly repeat these words: the Idea, the Cause..., who believe that tomorrow will bring something new and great, who by necessity ignore and despise the deep thinker, who bow to Vigny's "harrow-mob". The inner life and social action are mutually exclusive, and it is not given for them to understand each other. As an antithesis, read on one hand Schopenhauer's book *Wisdom in Life*, this bible of reserved, defiant and sad individualism, or Amiel's *Journal*, or Vigny's *Journal of a Poet*; on the other hand, read Benoît Malon, Elisée Reclus or Peter Kropotkin, and you will see the true dimensions of the gulf that lies between the two types of souls.

If one were now to ask about the salient traits of the anarchists' dogmatism, one might respond that the first and most important of these traits is intellectualism or scientism. Whatever the differences between orthodox Marxism and traditional anarchism might be, we may consider them, in Édouard Berth's great line, as "two divergent but complementary aspects of one and the same social psychology, of that very intellectualist and very rationalist social psychology which reigned in the second half of the last century[78]. What characterizes anarchism is its faith in science. The anarchists are in general great readers, fervent supporters of science. It is also a faith in the potential for science to found a rational society. Berth continues:

> Nobody is more fervently devoted to Science, and nobody has more belief in the virtue of science or is more ardent in this faith than the individualist anarchists are. They have always opposed Science to Religion and conceived Free-thought as a kind of anti-Church... But we must focus on this religion of Science, which is so highly developed among the individualist anarchists. There are two parties in Science: the one formal, abstract, systematic, dogmatic, a sort of metaphysical cosmology, far removed from the real world and yet claiming to encapsulate this diverse

[78] Berth, "Anarchisme individualiste, marxisme orthodoxe, syndicalisme révolutionnaire" (*Mouvement socialiste*, 1 May 1905)

and prodigiously complex real world in the unity of its abstract and simple formulas; it is *Science full stop, and with a capital S*; *unified* Science, claiming to strike a blow at Religion, to set solution against solution and provide the world and its origins with a rational explanation, — and then there are the sciences, diverse, concrete, each having its own methodology, adapted to its particular object, sciences that cleave as close as possible to the real world and become little more than *rationalized techniques.* Here, the so-called *unity of the sciences* is shattered. It is self-evident that the formal and metaphysical part is what the anarchists cultivate. It supplies an intellectual intoxication for its devotees, leading to strong illusions of power. It replaces religion, it fills the void left in the soul by their former faith. They inherit the Earth; they hold it with a few simple and clear formulas: what great might! and what great vengeance for isolated, solitary, and savage people! They escape the weakness and misery inherent in their solitude, and become masters of the Universe[79]!

From this scientistic intellectualism flows the anarchist's authoritarianism.

---

[79] Berth, *loc. cit.*, p. 14

Anarchist intellectualism — for it does not escape the law of all intellectualisms — thus terminates in the most perfect authoritarianism. This is its fatal flaw. There is no room for liberty in any kind of intellectualist system. Liberty is invention, the right and the power to find something new, to add something new to the universe: but when there is only one universal truth, which is revealed to us by religion or science, outside of which there is neither any individual happiness, nor any social order, liberty has no *raison d'être*, it only exists as a negative; science claims its liberty against religion, and when science is dominant, religion claims liberty against science, but, since two single and universal truths cannot both exist, one must annihilate its rival; for, if there is a truth, it is in the name of this one truth that social unity, moral unity, and national, international, human unity must be realized[80].

Scientistic intellectualism has left its imprint on every plan for social reorganization according to the anarchistic formulas. The first theoreticians of anarchy appeal to cosmological, physical, biological considerations, as pretentious as they are cloudy[81]. Biology is especially invoked for

---

[80] Berth, *loc. cit.*, p. 14

[81] On this point, see an issue of *la Plume* dating from the heroic time of the anarchy (May 1893). This issue contains

every purpose in support of the anarchistic utopias. It biology they point to, pointing out with living examples the spectacle of "autonomy

---

a theoretical exposition of the scientific bases of anarchism by André Veydaux and a plan for the future society from the economic, political, sexual, moral, and other perspectives, written by the principal anarchist writers of the epoch. Here is an example of the pseudo-scientific dreams of André Veydaux, where he leans on the authority of Lanessan: "The atom moves freely in its sphere, balanced by the gravitation of the ambient atomism. The testimony of nature is irrecusable. Minerality, vegetality, animality present in their intimate manifestations the spectacle of harmony in autonomy." ... "Does centralization really exist in multi-cellular creatures? Are their cells divided into dominant and obedient cells, into masters and subjects? All the facts that we know of respond negatively with the greatest of clarity. I will not focus on the real autonomy which each of the cells of every multi-cellular organism enjoys; for, if it is true that all of them depend on each other, it is also true that none of them commands the rest and that even the most highly developed multi-cellular organisms contain nothing comparable to a monarchy nor to every other authoritarian and centralized government. Autonomy and solidarity, such would be the basis of a society that would have been constructed according to the model of living beings... (De Lanessan, le Transformisme). "Society," continues M. A. Veydaux, will function from the individual to polymorphic, occasional, mobile, groups; from the groupings to the bundling of homologous and equivalent groupings, and so on to extreme association; this will be the free play of individualities; this will be variety in unity; for it is the public spectacle of natural harmony, it is the law of evolution, it is the condition sine qua non of the existence of human societies." Further on the theoretician becomes a poet as well: Tous bateaux ont bien libre jeu en meme port, / Pesant sur l'eau d'un proportionnel effort; / Par le gros vaisseau l'esquif est-il étouffé? (*La Plume*, May 1893) in harmony", inviting us to realize this ideal in human societies. It is she who suggests to us the egalitarian ideal of the equivalence of the functions of the organs in biological organisms and, by analogy, in the social organism. The vague ideal of evolution intervenes like a *deus ex machina* to resolve all difficulties. — It is likewise from the progress of science that anticipate the future welfare of humanity. Scientific and technological progress will engender such an overflowing of wealth that for people to snatch as they please from the general storehouse will be an adequate means of redistribution[82].

It goes without saying that individualism does not hold to any of these pseudo-scientific fantasies. For the individualist, Science does not exist; only sciences exist, that is to say, methods of investigation that are clever and sure to varying degrees. Nothing is more contrary to the true scientific spirit as the unitary scientism which has been discussed above. — Additionally, the individualist is at best a wary friend of intellectualism, where he rightly perceives the threat of authoritarianism. Along with Bayle,

---

[82] It is this famous layabout communism that Proudhon attacked in advance, in his famous pamphlet, *Droit a la Paresse*

Stendhal, and Fourier, he happily denies the power of ideas over our behavior; he limits his field of foresight, preferring liberty and chance. Foresight forges manacles for us; it makes us prudent, fearful, and calculating. The individualist is happy to join with Stirner in the happy song of the liberty of the moment; he suspects every sociological generalization, which, as an inexact science, is no less despotic for all that; he rebels against the oligarchy of savants fantasized by Berthelot with vanity to rival that of the ancient Popes when they imagined a universal theocracy. The individualist is not fond of the various plans for social reorganization; his attitude in the face of these problems is the fully negative one, as defined by Barrès in *l'Ennemi des lois*:

> What will you put in its place, you ask? I do not know, although I am quite curious on that point. Brought to the destruction of everything that is, I can't think of anything in particular to replace it with. It's like when someone's sore from boots that pinch: his only concern is to get them off... In all sincerity, I believe myself to belong to a race which is only good for understanding and disorganizing things[83].

---

[83] Barrès, *l'Ennemi des lois*, p. 25

* * *

The theoretical differences between anarchism and individualism lead to further ones in the practical sphere.

The course of action recommended by individualism relative to established society diverges widely from what anarchism prescribes.

For the individualist, the problem is the following: How can one live in a society which is viewed as, at best, a necessary evil?

It would seem that the radical solutions suggested by social pessimism are either to kill oneself or to retreat into the woods. But if, for better or worse, the individualist resists these extremes, a third solution comes to him, one that is not more radical, but only near and relative, and based on accommodation to the necessities of practical life. — The problem here is like what Schopenhauer posed at the beginning of his book *Wisdom in Life*. For him the issue is to establish an art of making life as agreeable and happy as possible, or, in his words, a "eudemonology." However, the idea of such a eudemonology stands in direct opposition to Schopenhauer's general conception of life. The eudemonology he offers is presented as an avowedly inferior philosophy, an "exoteric" one, suited to a mistaken perspective, a concession to human weakness and the necessities of practical life. As Schopenhauer said:

> To be capable of dealing with this issue, I have had to distance myself entirely from the elevated, metaphysical and moral point of view, to which my true philosophy points. All the developments that follow are therefore founded, to a certain degree, on an accommodation, in the sense that they are suited to the habitual, empirical point of view, and they preserve its errors[84].

In exactly the same way, it is licit for the individualist, from the social point of view, to ask himself what he can do to maximize his relative independence, in face of a social state that is necessarily oppressive and tyrannical. There is a practical problem that consists in relaxing, as far as possible, the social chains, in maximally

---

[84] Schopenhauer, *Wisdom in Life*, Introduction

slackening the encumbrances that society inflicts on the individual, in establishing a kind of deal and a tolerable *modus vivendi* for the individual who is condemned to live within society.

The tactical approach of the individualist against society is infinitely more complex, more delicate, more rich, more nuanced and more varied than the vulgar and brutal maxims of anarchism. — Here, everyone must make their own individual plan for life, must write their own rulebook, to help them maneuver in society, to escape it as far as possible, to escape the all-encompassing net, or rather, to slide past the social pitfalls, leaving as little flesh as possible on the thorns that line the path.

This tactical approach can work in two ways: first, in favor of the external liberation of the individual relative to those social relations and influences in which he finds himself engaged (social circles and the authorities on which he depends); and secondly, as a method of internal liberation or intellectual and moral lifestyle capable of strengthening one's feelings of independence and individuality.

On the first point, one might put the observations and the precepts of individualist moralists to use, establishing a small program which would consist of the following articles:

a. To minimize, as far as possible, external relations and subjugation. To facilitate this, to simplify one's life; not to undertake any relationship, nor affiliate with any group (leagues, parties, groupings of every kind) that might curtail our liberty at all (a precept from Descartes). To courageously brave the *via soli.* That is often useful;

b. If the lack of economic independence or some necessity to protect ourselves against more powerful and threatening influences compels us to undertake these relationships, not to tie ourselves except in an absolutely conditional and revocable way, and only to the degree ordained by our selfish interest;

c. To practice, against influences and powers, the defensive tactic which may be formulated like this: *Divide ut liber sis*[85].

Set the influences and rival powers against each other; carefully maintain their rivalries and prevent their collusion, which are always dangerous for the individual. To lean as often on one as on its rival, in such a way as to weaken and neutralize each by its opposite. Amiel recognized the fortunate effects of this tactic. "All political parties," he said, "aim equally at absolutism, at dictatorial omnipotence. Happily they are many; and we can set them against each other[86]";

d. By virtue of this see-saw tactic, when any one power gains too great a preponderance, it becomes, and rightly so, the enemy. From this point of view, individualism can certainly allow the existence of the State, but only a weak State, whose existence is precarious and threatened to the extent that it has to spare individuals;

e. To accommodate oneself outwardly to the laws and customs which are unavoidable. Not to overtly deny the

---

[85] Translator's note: "Divide the enemy and you are free"
[86] Amiel, *Journal intime,* II, p. 88

social pact; to deal with it only when one is the weaker party. The individualist, according to Remy de Gourmont, is he who "denies, that is to say, destroys as far as he can, the principle of authority. He it is who, every time he can do so without harm, will escape every law and social obligation with a clear conscience. He denies and destroys authority in what concerns him personally; he becomes as free as a man can be in our complex societies[87]".

The precepts relating to the political attitude deserve special attention. In principle, individualism is indifferent to all political regimes, in that it is hostile to all of them. The ruling idea of *Stello* is that all political regimes: monarchy (See his *Histoire d'une puce enragée*), a bourgeois republic (*Histoire de Chatterton*), Jacobin republics (*Une Histoire de la Terreur*), all equally persecute the poets, in other words, the superior, genial, and independent individualities. "Thus," says Stello, noticing this perpetual ostracism, "Power can take three possible forms: the first fears us, the second disdains us as useless, the third hates us and

---

[87] Rémy de Gourmont, *Épilogues*, II

would try to level us as arrogant aristocrats. Shall we be the eternal helots of society?" Thoreau refused to vote and called politics "something unreal, incredible, and insignificant." The fact remains that the individual can usefully engage in politics. It can be a means of combating and neutralizing other social influences from which it suffers. — On the other hand, by the very fact that, in principle, it is equally defiant of all regimes, individualism can, in practice, accommodate itself to all of them and find reconciliation with all opinions[88].

Some individualists are particularly harsh on democracy. Others are inspired by Bergeret, who rallies to it as the least dogmatic and least

---

[88] It is perhaps from this perspective that it is possible to reconcile the political conservatism of Barres with his individualistic ideas as developed in *Un Homme libre* and *l'Ennemi des lois*. Maybe Barrès is also playing the see-saw which consists in treating the strongest party as his enemy. Or, maybe, he obeys some apprehension of his artistic sensibility. Seeing, rightly or wrongly, in ascendant socialism the coming of a barbarity that will be fatal for individuality and art, he seeks refuge, always by the same see-saw tactic, in the more rigidly conservative and traditionalist party. — It might be apt to add, moreover, that Barrès's individualistic attitude is not always perfectly clear. If he seems very much the individualist in *l'Ennemi des lois* and *Un Homme libre*, on the other hand, in a curious minor work entitled *De Hegel aux cantines du Nord*, he seems to recommend a true federalist anarchism

unitary regime: "Democracy," says Bergeret, "is still the regime and I prefer. With it, all bonds are relaxed, which weakens the State, while sheltering persons, and it procures a certain facility of living with a liberty which miserably destroys the local tyrannies."

Aside from the external tactics discussed above, a method, a daily routine of intellectual and moral practice comes to the fore, aiming to maintain our inner independence. It may also be summarized by these few precepts:

> *a.* Cultivate in oneself social skepticism, social dilettantism, and all the mental attitudes that result from individualism;

> *b.* Remain fully conscious of the precarious, fictive[89], and, at bottom, optional character of the social pact and of the individual's need to rectify all that is overly tyrannical in this pact, by every trick of the most tolerant and expansive individualistic casuistic;

---

[89] See Dr. Toulouse's article entitled, "Le Pacte social" (*Journal*, July 1905)

c. To meditate and follow Descartes's precept, writing of his stay in Holland: "I walk among men as if they were trees." To isolate oneself, to withdraw into oneself, to see those around us as if they were trees in a forest; here you see a true individualistic attitude;

d. To meditate and observe Vigny's precept: "To separate the poetic life from the political life": thus dividing the true life, the life of thought and feelings, from the external and social life;

e. To practice Fourier's dual rule: *Absolute doubt* (with respect to civilization), and *Absolute isolation* (from the traditional and well-beaten paths);

f. To meditate and observe Emerson's precept: "Never let yourself be chained by the past, either in deed or in thought";

g. For that, to lose no chance to shrug off the habitual social influences, and to flee all social crystallization. Most of everyday experience shows how important this precept truly is. When we have passed some time in a narrow milieu which circumvents and whose pettiness, petty criticisms, miniscule dangers and petty hatreds start to grate on us, nothing is better at setting our feelings and our true selves in relief than a short vacation, a brief trip somewhere else. Then we can feel how much we were, as if unconsciously, harnessed and tamed by society. We return with our eyes opened, our head refreshed and cleared from all the petty social stupidity that had infected it. At other times, if travel is impossible, we can at least escape into great art. I recall a friend who was ill and isolated in nasty, small town, surrounded by petty feuds and idiotic gossips, found infinite sensations of joy and liberty by re-reading *Reisebilder* novels. He escaped with Heine into an enchanted dream-world, while the real world ceased to exist for him.

These individualist precepts are only meant as examples. We find a great number of similar ones in Schopenhauer's *Wisdom in Life* and also in Vigny and Stirner. It is enough for my purposes here to have exposed the individualist's psychology and to have distinguished it from that of the anarchist.

* * *

Let us say a word, by way of conclusion, on the probable destinies of anarchism and individualism.

At the present hour, anarchism seems to have entered, either as a doctrine, or as a party, into a period of disintegration and dissolution. Laurent Tailhade, who truly is a turncoat of their party, once noticed this dissolution with a combination of melancholy and irony. The reason behind this disintegration is likely found in the intimate contradictions that we have noted above. That is, the contradiction that subsists between the two principles which anarchism claims to reconcile: the individualist or libertarian principle and the humanist or solidarist principle, which is translated on the economic plane as communism. By the very evolution of the doctrine, these two elements gradually tend to disassociate from each other. With a certain number of anarchists (especially the intellectuals), we can see anarchism transforming more or less neatly into pure and simple individualism, that is to say, into a mental attitude that is very different from anarchism properly speaking, and compatible, as needed, with the acceptance of political and social institutions far removed from the traditional anarchist ideal. Others, in greater numbers, above all those who place greatest weight on matters of material life and economic organization, cheapen individualism and gleefully denounce it as the fancy of aristocrats and an unbearable selfishness. Their anarchism ends in an extreme socialism, to a kind of humanitarian and egalitarian communism and which leaves no room for individualism. — Thus, in anarchism an antagonism of principles and tendencies appears, which constitute the inescapable seeds of its disintegration[90].

---

[90] Fouillée, in his book *Nietzsche et l'Immoralisme*, traces the current evolution of anarchism and points to the conflict between individualistic tendency as with Stirner, and the humanitarian tendency that is translated on the metaphysical terrain by a naturalist monism, as in Spinoza. Having cited a passage from Reclaire, Stirner's translator, who pretends to substitute for the Stirnerite conception of the "Unique" one that of a common and universal self, a "common depth" of individualities, Fouillée adds: "It is well know that theoretical anarchism has in our days ended up as a monism as in Spinoza and as with Schopenhauer: *The Unique One*, who was at first only an individual and an ego, has become in this *common ground of all*, of which "Science" furnishes us a glimpse, that "Philosophy" alone can extricate for us. The Unique One, "The All-One". (Fouillée. *Nietzsche et l'Immoralisme*,

Individualism as we have defined it, — the sense of revolt against social constraint, the sense of the uniqueness of the self, the sense of the contradictions that inevitably arise in every social state between the individual and the society, the social pessimism — individualism, I say, would not seem on the point of disappearing from the soul of contemporary man. It has found, in modern times, more than one sincere and impassioned interpreter, whose voice will yet find an echo, for a long time, in souls enamored of independence. Individualism does not have the passing and artificial character of a political and social doctrine, as anarchism does. The reasons for its perennial relevance are psychological rather than social. In spite of the predictions of the optimistic sociologists, who, like Draghicesco[91], are persuaded that the path of social evolution and the mechanical functioning of certain simple laws, including the law of social integration, will have the power, in the near or distant future, of fully rationalizing and socializing the human instincts, of assimilating, equalizing, and domesticating every soul, of drowning the individual in the collective, of scrubbing him clean from his every wish for individuality, his every longing for independence and of resistance against the so-called law of reason and morality, finally leading to the advent

p. 8, F. Alcan.)
[91] *l'Individu dans le Déterminisme social*

of the race of "happy cowards" mentioned by Leconte de Lisle, we may believe that individualism will remain a permanent and indestructible form of human sensibility, and that it will be with us as long as societies themselves last.

THE MORAL ANTINOMY BETWEEN THE INDIVIDUAL AND SOCIETY

From *Les antinomies entre l'individu et la societé* (1913)

Morality is the idealized expression of the social instinct. The moral contradiction between the individual and society recapitulates and crowns all other such contradictions.

Morality is the great enemy of individuality. It tries, either by imperious directives or by persuasion, to make the individual deny himself. It would like to abolish every feeling of individuality, because these always have, virtually at least, something antisocial in them; because they are a point of origin for diversity and struggle, the point of origin of resistance and of disobedience. — Doubtless, since man is a complex being, and since there are two inimical souls in him: the social and the individual souls, morality must take special account of this duality and make certain concessions to the feeling of individuality. We find here and there in the moral doctrines, particularly in the Stoic and Kantian moralities, an appeal to the ideal of personality, to the ideals of individual liberty and individual autonomy. But if we look more closely, we quickly realize that the personality glorified by moralists is always, at bottom, "the ideal essence of humanity", or "impersonal reason", or "the unitary aspect, identical in all individuals". At bottom, the idea of personality is only ever evoked formulaically. The praises we sing to it are Platonic in character. Its only place in the ethical theories is analogous to the statues of the Buddha in Chinese temples: incense is burned to them, but otherwise they are disregarded.

All the moralities, then, repeat this mantra to the individual: "Don't think you have any importance. Admit your nothingness and insignificance. Sacrifice yourself to society, which is infinitely greater, more durable, more fertile, more powerful and more beautiful than you are. If you find modern society imperfect and unworthy of your sacrifice, at least give yourself to an ideal society that will one day materialize, for which your sacrifice will have paved the way." Every morality is part of the system of social illusions that I have described elsewhere; or rather it is its centerpiece. The moralities lead the individual to play the man gladly gives his neck to the executioner. There is no end to the forms of the moralists' cunning. The spiritualist illusion consists in exploiting the survival instinct of the individual. Religions and moralities offer a conditional immortality to the individual. They give him this ultimatum:

"Survive? Yes, you'll survive... if you obey." The Messianic illusion that reappears in the secular and humanitarian moralities differs in no way from the preceding illusion. "Sacrifice yourself," the individual is told; "do not rebel against unjust society; justice will reign one day." — As if this promise were not derisive and insulting to the very idea of justice that is invoked. For if justice is ever realized, it will not have any retroactive efficacy; the future will not redeem the past and the contrast between the perfection of the future state and the existing imperfection will only make the past and its irreparable injustices more painful. — Spiritualism and Messianism are two "stages of illusion", as de Hartmann has written. The other moral ideologies: the ideology of the "general interest", the "general will", or the "general happiness", are based on the same illusory principles, and from the perspective of an ultimate harmony which enchants the soul and bends them to the laws of society. At the bottom of each of these ideologies we find the same sophisms, the same circular reasoning. That which is in question is presupposed, when it's maintained that the *true interest*, the *true happiness* of an individual consists in his doing what is useful for society; and that therefore, every individual who acts differently is declared to be chasing a *false happiness*, who must be prevented from harming themselves and others in this way. The "general will", the "general interest", "solidarity": these are all so many ideological phantoms which haunt and dominate the individual with their fearsome shadows, like the "specter of Religion" mentioned by Lucretius.

The theory of unitary and absolute Duty is another ethical lie, which is presupposed and claimed by the preceding ones. In fact, however, we find nothing like a unitary and absolute duty; but rather with multiple and relative duties, which are often divergent or even mutually antagonistic. We can never fulfill any given duty except by violating many other ones. The duty of serving my family and friends contravenes my duty to be just to all. My duty to respect authority often contravenes my duty to the truth. The worker who is on strike is caught between duty to his family and duty to his union. These conflicts usually come from the fact that the individual belongs to multiple groups whose interests are not always consonant.

The moralists cannot deny these conflicts; but they do not like to waste their energy on this matter. They generally have little taste for that casuistry which unfortunately emphasizes the imperfections of social solidarity, the contradictions and uncertainties in ethics; thereby inviting the individual to examine his duty more closely, to discuss and deal with it. The study of individual cases of consciousness leads people to individualize morality, to recognize that there are as many moralities as there are individuals; it is not only duty which varies according to the particular situation. This is why nearly every moralist accepts that it is best not to reflect too much about one's duty, but that it should be accepted and fulfilled without discussion or examination. When the moralists consent to examine these difficulties, their solution consists in arbitrarily selecting a single one of the individual's duties, considering it in isolation and holding it as absolutely sacred. The other duties will become what they can. But above all, again, keep them away from all discussion. Discussion about morality is a pretext under which the selfish instinct is surreptitiously resisting the social instinct and subverting the rules.

A triple influence has contributed or contributes to the discredit which today strikes at this casuistry: the influence of university thought; that of politicians' thought, and that of workers' thought, currently represents the final term of democratic thought.

University thought, imbued with Kantian rigor, is the natural enemy of this casuistry.

What is more, the university moralists, operating as they do in the ideal and the abstract, moreover, not being burdened professionally with overseeing and guiding ethical practice, feel no obligation, as our "directors of conscience" once did, to make their morality practicable, to adapt it to the diversity of circumstances and the demands of human weakness. It is natural that those who stop at theory will teach an austere, elevated, difficult, and beautiful morality.

The politician's spirit, which permeates everything nowadays, thus has something to do with the discrediting of this casuistry. Politicians in a democracy are gleefully simplistic, absolutist, and dogmatic. Such minds find it scandalous to dispute about their duty and thereby cast doubt on the infallibility of conscience and the certainty of the law. In their view, we must obey the law without discussion and without examination; the moral law as well as the civil law. — Moral rigorism has, finally, also found support outside the University and the politicians, among the working classes. If, on some points, socialism is of a certain sensualist and materialist inspiration, it inclines no less towards a rigid, violent and authoritarian moralism. The worker imbued with class consciousness forms an absolute and intransigent conception of his duty. Georges Sorel has demonstrated the existence of a latent moral "sublime" in the soul of the laborer; of an aptitude for sacrifice in the merciless struggle, which the working class maintains against the possessing classes, whom it identifies with immortality. — The anti-clerical working-class man gladly confuses this casuistry with Jesuitism; what is more, he is intolerant of all unseemly conduct and opinion, and he has no respect whatsoever for individual liberty.

Moreover, the latter reason is the more profound reason, which one finds at the bottom of all the rest. The enemies of this casuistry take it for a sophistry in the service of the instinct of liberty and moral lawlessness; as a pretext which the selfish instinct is too ready to call on, which is always eager to escape the authority of the rules. The great grievance held for this casuistry is less of its often bringing dubious solutions than of having posed disquieting problems and of honoring debate on morality. If anyone enters a debate about duty, they are already regarded as shirking their duty; it is already a beginning of moral lawlessness and immoralism.

The anti-individualist tendency of every ethical system is maximally and most clearly expressed in the last-comer of moral theories, ethics — the science of morals, or the scientific morality, or the sociological morality which may also be called the "sociocratic" morality.

It is true that this morality renounces the idea of a unitary and universal duty. It allows a certain moral relativism by reason of the diversity of "social types". But within the limits of a given "social type", certain rules of morality are imposed on the individual with the need for certain objective constraints. For Durkheim, moral rules express a sovereign and omnipotent power before which the individual must only prostrate himself. The will of Jehovah is replaced by that of the group.

Lucien Lévy-Brühl says that that the "art of morality" as deduced from sociology will not be imperative like religions and moral metaphysics have been. It will not intimate any orders; it will proceed by slow pressure upon public opinion, by propaganda, by exhortation and advice. — This amounts to saying that the art of morality will be a persuasive, and not an imperative morality. So be it, but, as Faguet remarks, the art of morality, basing itself on scientific observation, on statistics, etc., will eventually be declared scientific; it will nominate itself "the scientific art of morality" and will assume a rather arrogant authority, which everything that is either scientific or has such pretentions always does. "Moral art would not be imperative; but as off-putting as this may be, I'd wager on it becoming so[92]."

On his side, Albert Bayet shows a tendency to restrict the field of action of the scientific art of morality and to remove a significant part of the individual life from its purview. As this moralist sees things, there is an entire part of our being, the intimate part, the interior life, the life of thought and feeling, at which "the scientific art of morality" must halt.

The art of morality will only reach the social parts of man. The truly individual part, the heart of hearts, is beyond its reach. Bayet leaves for each the faculty of cultivating, at his own risk and peril, his "secret garden". — "The art of society," he says, "will abstain from intervening in the sorrowful hours of the interior life. It will

---

[92] E. Faguet. *La démission de la morale*, p. 241

leave to each their sufferings great or small, humble or tragic, intolerable or light, long-lasting or fleeting; for none of the interests which he is pursuing is incompatible with the forms that an individual's pain can assume[93]."

This reservation in favor of the individual's heart of hearts show's Bayet's liberal-mindedness, but it does not seem to fit with the general trajectory of the "sociocratic morality". It is consistent with this morality to try and penetrate, in spite of everything, to the most intimate parts of the mind and the heart. In effect, the commonplace of the moralists on the close solidarity joining the inner life of the individual to his external and social conduct. It is declared that there is not a single one of our thoughts or feelings which lacks its repercussions, whether direct or indirect, on our conduct and thereby on our environment. — Consequently, how can the art of morality fail to take an interest in the interior life, in the "secret garden" of the individual? For it is in this secret garden where the seeds take root, which will blossom in the great public garden of social life. Will the art of society recognize the right to self-expression of thoughts which are plainly antisocial, or judged such (for example, a-social or anti-social pessimism, or immoralism)? I doubt it. Here the convenient principle of the "normal direction" of the collective conscience intervenes, and such internal dispositions are declared to be out of sync with the so-called

[93] Albert Bayet, *La morale scientifique*

"normal direction". That would be all too easy; for the principle of normal direction implies, at bottom, an obligation to think like everyone else.

Bayet's concession to individual autonomy is likewise precarious and always subject to retraction. In effect, Bayet declares that, in principle, every time a conflict arises between the interests of the group and those of the individual, the former can be preferred as the interest of all, even in certain respects of those it may harm[94]. — Once this principle is granted, the interior life itself, as far as it has consequences for the social life, is a great risk of falling entirely within the grasp of social regulation; moreover, from the very moment when the external conduct of the individual is subject to this regulation, isn't it merely a Platonic concession to grant people the liberty of their deepest self? At bottom, this is like leaving people's eyes in so they can cry.

The sociological morality, while claiming to be scientific and objective, is faithful to its own logic where it claims to eliminate the personal factor from morality, along with personal judgment, reflection, and individual decision-making. But this essential point is also the most dubious one. The partisans of the sociological morality forget that the moral problem is a problem of values, and that problems like these cannot be solved through purely objective considerations. Problems of values imply a subjective element: a

---

[94] Bayet, loc. cit., p. 170

judgment brought by the individual, a judgment which is added to the facts; a personal preference, assigning qualities to them. In all this there is an "arbitrary addition[95]", an "internal movement", which dictates personal evaluations to the individual.

This is why the moral solutions are no less aleatory in character among the scientific morality than in any other morality. Solidarity or liberty, equality or inequality, resignation or revolt, moralism or immoralism; or, to pass on to more particular problems, indissoluble marriage or facilitated divorce, condemnation or legitimization of suicide: there are as many problems as ambiguous solutions, which are decided by the individual's judgment, and in all truth, at bottom, the individual's temperament.

This is so striking that even the partisans of the scientific morality do not agree among themselves on many issues. Durkheim, for example, is against easing any restrictions on divorce; Bayet is for divorce by the consent of a single party. Durkheim loathes suicide as an attack against society and against humanity: Bayet allows it as an evident right of the individual.

---

[95] The expression comes from Delbos: "The objective science of customs cannot produce any definite rule nor prescribe to the will what goals it should take — *unless by an arbitrary addition.*"

In the facts of morality, there is too much contingency at work for anyone to eliminate the personal factor. It is individual evaluations which, in the final analysis, judges between good and evil.

In sum, the sociocratic morality, whose partisans are at war with the ancient meta-moralities, is itself a meta-morality. It joins the ancient meta-moralities in presupposing a metaphysical postulate, i.e., a subjective one, which leads the collective will to trample on the individual will, even to annihilate the latter for the good of the former. The ancient theological precept: "obey the will of God" is replaced by the sociocratic precept, which is no less metaphysical than its predecessor: "obey the will of the group".

Against the sociocratic aims of these moralities, the protest of the individual who wants to be himself, who wants to draw on his own feelings and his own reasons for acting, and not to find them in religious beliefs or social imperatives; this protest of individuality may take two forms. — There is a negative individualism which is pure and simple immoralism, the negation of every moral idea considered as a prejudice aiming to subjugate the individual. The brutal and cynical immoralism of Stirner; the refined and mocking immoralism of the social dilettante are the two forms of this individualism. — There is also an aristocratic individualism which is not, *prima facie*, as clearly antisocial as the first, but which necessarily goes that way in the end. This individualism denies the social morality that is currently dominant, and maybe even social morality as such; it denies it as a morality for the weak, the mediocre, the cowardly, cheats, hypocrites, and traitors; deception and treason being a form of weakness (recall the treachery of women. Many men are women too, in this way); it denies all of it as a morality of the envious, of those who resent all strength and superiority, a morality of conformists, both servile and intolerant. For them, herd-life is necessary because this is where such virtues as they are capable of will fare best, and because they cannot fail to despise a strong spirit, when they sense its power and greatness. — But above this miserable morality, which resents all strength, greatness, and individualized beauty which affirms itself as independent from the herd, the aristocrat conceives a morality made for him and the few who are like him, his equals; a morality of the superman, a morality which, moreover, each superman will conceive in his own way, in his own image, inspired by his own ideal. This morality also show itself to have, with its various representatives, several traits in common; it is individualistic in each case. By this I mean that it glorifies individual forces; it rises against the gregarious coalitions which seek to oppress by sheer force of numbers. With nearly all of its representatives it glorifies sincerity, noble frankness which accompanies strength; the courage which loves and seeks individual responsibility, which does not shelter behind anyone else.

Les animaux laches vont en troupe
Le lion marche seul dans le désert
Qu'ainsi marche toujours le poete[96].

Above all, Vigny focuses on the qualities of moral frankness and independence. Gobineau, on the qualities of independence and intelligent energy; Nietzsche glorifies savage and untamed power, the will-to-power of the masters, which is both destructive and creative, which renews the world, often at the price of terrible convulsions and bloody sacrifices. Ibsen glorifies the courageous intelligence which breaks the old civilizational molds, trampling on outdated prejudices, and builds a fresh and new truth on their ruins, even though this too is destined to age and perish. Beyond these differences in ideals, one value remains constant: that of the noble personality, the strongly individualized personality, which is opposed to the mediocre and servile mob.

In truth, this morality does not exclude, in any absolute way, an idea of society and of sociability. Often, it even seems to aspire to a superior sociability, exempt from hypocrisy, enamored of intelligence and science (Vigny, *La bouteille a la mer*; *Le pur Esprit*); empowered by knowledge and enlarged solidarity (Ibsen, *Enemy of the People*). But to tell the truth, these

---

[96] The cowardly animals go in a troop / The lion stalks alone in the desert / May the poet always go that way too! - Vigny, *Journal d'un poète*

wishes for sociability, these hopes for sociability, or these concessions to sociability are rare and precarious; quickly vanquished by the individualist and antisocial sentiment which is at the base of the aristocratic morality.

The virtues recommended or glorified by the great aristocrats are not the properly moral virtues, the Christian virtues or even stoic ones (except sometimes with Vigny); they are the virtues of strength: conquering virtues, amoral virtues. Aristocratic individualism does not represent the superiority of the individual as any sort of moral superiority (a Christian or Stoic point of view, virtues of devotion, of sacrifice, of abnegation); instead it represents a superiority of strength, intelligence, independent energy: all the faculties that are not properly moral (the standpoint of Gobineau, Ibsen, and Nietzsche). The attitude of the aristocrat is thus naturally oriented towards an amoral and antisocial individualism. For, when the aristocrat comes into conflict with society, he will always prefer himself to society; he will prefer his own ideal, i.e. the reflection of his personality, to the social ideal which for him is mediocre, false and degraded. And this conflict is inevitable. The herd naturally detests aristocrats, and the gregarious morality resists aristocracy. The latter meets with resistance from mute and hypocritical hostilities, or even a force of inertia, and from the brutish indifference that discourages all pioneers.

The creator of thoughts perceives that they fall on an ungrateful ground and that by falling they lose their best qualities. The aristocrat eventually loses faith: if not in his own thoughts, at least in their social efficacy; the only refuge he finds is in the pessimistic individualism of which Vigny and Gobineau remain the perfect representatives, in the ivory tower of the misanthropic thinker, where wounded minds find their final, arrogant, and silent shelter.

Lightning Source UK Ltd.
Milton Keynes UK
UKHW011205280621
386285UK00004B/1360